C000021051

WINNERS

HORSES TO FOLLOW – FLAT 2022

Sixtieth year of publication

Contributors:
Rodney Pettinga
Richard Young

RACING POST

First published by Pitch Publishing on behalf of Racing Post, 2022

Pitch Publishing, 9 Donnington Park, 85 Birdham Road,
Chichester, West Sussex, PO20 7AJ

www.pitchpublishing.co.uk
info@pitchpublishing.co.uk
www.racingpost.com/shop

Order line: 01933 304 858

Copyright © 2022, Pitch Publishing and Racing Post

Every effort has been made to trace the copyright. Any oversight will be
rectified in future editions at the earliest opportunity by the publisher.

All rights reserved. No part of this book may be reproduced, sold or utilised
in any form or transmitted in any form or by any means, electronic or
mechanical, including photocopying, recording or by any information storage
and retrieval system, without prior permission in writing from the Publisher.

A CIP catalogue record is available for this book
from the British Library.

ISBN 978-1-83950-096-1

Printed and bound in Great Britain by Streamline Press.

100 WINNERS

HORSES TO FOLLOW – FLAT 2022

(ages as at 2022)

A CASE OF YOU (IRE)

4 b c Hot Streak - Karjera (Key Of Luck)

A record of five wins from just 11 career outings, including
the Group 1 Prix De L'Abbaye on his penultimate start last
season, is a fine record for this four-year-old son of Hot
Streak and he should continue to make his presence felt in all
of the top sprints this coming season. He was initially tried
over 7f in April but finished last of 12 behind subsequent
2,000 Guineas winner Poetic Flare at Leopardstown, running
as if something was amiss (pulled hard), but he quickly made
amends by taking a Group 3 over 6f in May at Naas from
Mooneista (demoted to third), who would frank the form by
winning the Group 2 Sapphire Stakes subsequently. A big run
was expected in the Commonwealth Cup at Royal Ascot over
the same trip but A Case Of You lost a shoe as he finished
down the field behind Campanelle, who got the race in the
Steward's room. He ran a better race in a Group 3 next time
and he followed that with another much-improved run in the
Group 1 Flying Five Stakes at the Curragh in September, in
which he finished a close second behind Romantic Proposal.
He then provided trainer Adrian McGuinness with his first
Group 1 winner when scorching clear with one other horse
in the Prix de L'Abbaye, and he signed off with a respectable
fifth in the Grade 1 Breeders' Cup Sprint at Del Mar, where
he may not have been ideally suited by the fast ground. No
doubt this season will again be geared around races like the
Flying Five and the L'Abbaye, but he wouldn't look out of
place in the King's Stand or the Nunthorpe Stakes either.
ADRIAN MCGUINNESS

AADDEEY (IRE)

5 b g New Approach - Feedyah (Street Cry)

Given Aaddeey turned five in January, he's not had much racing, which lends hope to the theory that he may well have a bit of further improvement to come this year. He's already shown he's capable of smart form, having won handicaps at Newmarket and at Doncaster last year. He's pretty versatile ground-wise too, with the Newmarket victory coming on good ground while the latter success on his final 2021 outing was achieved on soft. That Doncaster victory – his first run in a tongue-tie – also showed he can cope admirably in a tactical race and he looks a fair bit better than the bare facts of that slowly run race after losing ground at the start and then being held up. He was raised to 103 on the back of that win and he's just the type to win a good-quality handicap this time round. Given his connections, it would be no surprise were he to be shipped out to contest a handicap or a minor Group event at the Dubai Carnival early this year.
SIMON & ED CRISFORD

ADAYAR (IRE)

4 b c Frankel - Anna Salai (Dubawi)

Charlie Appleby was appointed as a Godolphin trainer in 2013 (following the suspension of Mahmood Al Zarooni) after 15 years of working for Sheikh Mohammed in a variety of roles, including travelling head lad, stable head lad and assistant trainer. The approachable Newmarket handler reached the pinnacle of his relatively brief training career when topping last year's Flat trainer's championship with over 100 winners and prize money of almost £5 million. The biggest single contributor to that fund was Adayar, who won the English Derby in June to give Appleby his second win in the race since 2018. The strapping son of Frankel followed up that win by taking the all-aged King George VI and Queen Elizabeth over a month later, where a powerful display of galloping and a useful weight-for-age allowance proved too much for John & Thady Gosden's top-class colt Mishriff. Things didn't go to plan in his last two races – he was probably found out by the heavy ground in the Arc (though he ran respectably in fourth) while the season may have caught up with him when he underperformed in the Champion Stakes at Ascot on his final start in October. Everything about his physique suggests that he'll be an even better 4-y-o – especially if he can settle a bit better in the early stages of his races – and he'll be a strong contender for all the top prizes at around 1m4f. The Sheema Classic at Meydan on World Cup night could be a good starting point and a second King George could be the main target on the domestic front. CHARLIE APPLEBY

ALBAHR

3 ch g Dubawi – Falls Of Lora (Street Cry)

Albahr's juvenile season ended on a low note when he became trapped under the gates before the start of the Breeders' Cup Juvenile Turf in November, which meant he was withdrawn from the race. However, everything he had done until that point marked him out as a top 3-y-o prospect. He won two novice events at Haydock (both 7f) on his second and third starts in the summer (he was gelded in between those two runs) before taking the step up to Listed level in his stride in a 1m contest at Salisbury, drawing clear of the field with one other rival. He then improved again when sent to Woodbine in Canada to contest the Grade 1 Summer Stakes, in which he pulled nearly 3l clear from a solid benchmark in the shape of Grafton Street. That rival went on to be beaten by just 2l in the Juvenile Turf, from which Albahr had to be scratched, so it is fair to assume that he would have been involved in the finish but for that unfortunate incident at the gates. Appleby confirmed afterwards that his charge suffered only minor cuts and bruises and he was able to resume his career quickly at Meydan in January, although he was well beaten there in a conditions race over an inadequate 7f on dirt. He can surely bounce back from that and add to his tally in this country, especially as he steps up to 1m2f and beyond. CHARLIE APPLEBY

ANGEL BLEU (FR)

3 b c Dark Angel - Cercle De La Vie (Galileo)

The winner of five races from eight starts at two, including two Group 1s in October, Angel Bleu certainly had a busy time of it as a juvenile, but he improved in leaps and bounds once encountering soft/heavy ground towards the end of the season. Down the field in the Coventry Stakes (good to firm) in June and then second in a Listed race over 7f at Ascot (good to firm) the following month, his career took off just three days after that run when he beat Berkshire Shadow on soft ground in the Group 2 Vintage Stakes over 7f at Goodwood. He did plenty wrong too, as he got warm beforehand and raced very keenly, but he still outspeeded the runner-up to win a shade comfortably. He was then off until Arc day, where he contested the Prix Jean Luc Lagardere, again over 7f, and the heavy ground turned out to be ideal for him as he won with the minimum of fuss. Stepped up to 1m on his final run of the season, he won the Criterium International at Saint-Cloud, beating Ancient Rome, who had also finished behind him at Longchamp. That brought his record under Frankie Dettori to 2111, including those two Group 1s, and it now seems that he will be aimed at the Poule d'Essai des Poulains. Clearly, plenty of cut is important to Angel Bleu, but he's a tough cookie and, granted his ideal conditions, he will take plenty of stopping as a three-year-old. RALPH BECKETT

ANMAAT (IRE)

4 b g Awtaad - African Moonlight (Halling)

The death of Sheikh Hamdan Al Maktoum last year robbed the international racing world of one of its most prominent and influential supporters. The nine-time champion owner in Britain leaves a lasting legacy, and although the number of horses carrying his famous royal blue silks with white epaulettes and striped cap has been pruned back they will still be a familiar sight on racecourses up and down the country. One horse that could make his way into Pattern company in 2022 is Anmaat, who won a Lingfield maiden on his reappearance but who ended the season as a 103-rated performer. Ironically, his best effort came in defeat when he was run down in the closing stages of the competitive Cambridgeshire at Newmarket in September by Saeed Bin Suroor's talented but enigmatic Bedouin's Story. The way he travelled through the race and responded to pressure suggests strongly he should be able to make that transition into Group company and, as the 5-y-o has only had seven races, there should be a fair bit more improvement to come. He's a tactically versatile sort who should have no problems if connections elect either to drop him back to 1m or to return him to 1m2f. OWEN BURROWS

ARMOR

3 b c No Nay Never - Hestia (High Chaparral)

Generally progressive as a sprinter at two, Armor could easily land a big prize as he embarks on his 3-y-o career in 2022. He won two of his first three starts, a Doncaster maiden in April from a subsequent dual winner and the Group 3 Molecomb Stakes at Goodwood in July, which he won by three and a quarter lengths from Fearby. He maintained his good form afterwards without winning again – he twice finished behind Perfect Power in Group 1 races, firstly in the Prix Morny in August over 6f on good to soft, which seemed to stretch him, and then in the Middle Park Stakes in September, again over 6f, where he ran a personal best despite being beaten by just under a length. In between those runs he finished a neck second to Caturra in the Group 2 Flying Childers Stakes, where he was mugged on the line. After his run in the Middle Park, Richard Hannon was quoted as saying: 'I always felt if we knew he handled fast ground it would be worth taking him to the Breeders' Cup for the Juvenile Sprint. He is improving and developing more physically than I expected, so I would love to try for another Group 1 option.' He did run at Del Mar in early November but he missed the kick and, while he stayed on well in the closing stages to only be beaten by about 2l, he was never really in contention. There will be other days for him and he could easily break his Group 1 duck in the coming months, possibly over 7f or a mile.
RICHARD HANNON

ARTHUR'S VICTORY (IRE)
4 b f Buratino - Impressive Victory (Street Cry)

There's every chance that this filly, who won two races over 7f last summer, can progress again at four and win more races at a lowly level off her current mark of 73 at up to a mile. Having shown a degree of promise in her first four outings, she got off the mark at Epsom at the fifth time of asking in late July and, while it wasn't the strongest of races, she was always doing enough to hold off Apache Jewel, with a yawning 9l back to the third. She was upped in grade at Wolverhampton the following month and she passed the test with flying colours, getting up in the dying strides to deny Urtzi, with that pair pulling clear of the remainder. She was fancied to complete the hat-trick back at Epsom later that month, but she simply wasn't suited by how the race unfolded as the first four home were in the first four throughout and, while she made some strong late gains to finish on the heels of them, they weren't stopping quickly enough for her to trouble them. She wasn't seen again last year but there's still mileage in her current mark and, while she's no world-beater, she looks more than capable of adding to her tally, especially granted a truly run race. JOSEPH PARR

AZALLYA (IRE)
4 b f Le Havre - Azama (Sea The Stars)

Having shown promise over 1m2f in two starts in the early part of the season, this nicely bred Aga Khan filly ran three terrific races over 1m4f from June onwards, progressing markedly each time. Firstly, she finished a close third behind Call Me Sweetheart and Simply A Dream in a Curragh maiden in early June before getting off the mark at Cork on her next start in August, comfortably beating Cycladic, who would go on to win her maiden by six and a half lengths next time. Azallya, whose dam is a half-sister to the top-class Azamour, was stepped up to Listed company on her final start in October, but she ran a smashing race, finishing a half-length second of 16 to Jason The Militant, with more than 3l back to the third.

Still unexposed relative to many of her rivals, she showed there that she had made good progress since her maiden win and she will appeal to her owner/breeder as one who could stay in training at four with realistic prospects of winning a Listed or Group 3 contest. DERMOT WELD

BAAEED

4 b c Sea The Stars - Aghareed (Kingmambo)

In only six career starts Baaeed has catapulted himself to almost the top of the pile when it comes to Raceform Ratings (RRs) of horses sired by Sea The Stars, himself an outstanding 3-y-o over 1m2f–1m4f in 2009. Only Crystal Ocean of his progeny has achieved a higher RR than Baaeed at this stage, but that could change during the coming season, especially as the colt has a fair bit of physical scope for further improvement. Not too many had heard the name Baaeed when he made his debut at Leicester last June and he was allowed to go off at 6-1 to beat a field of maidens. Despite a slow start, he was well on top at the finish and he stepped up again when following up in a Newmarket novice less than a fortnight later. Such was the manner of that Newmarket win that he went off a shade of odds-on when upped to Listed company at the July meeting, where he created a lasting impression to beat Maximal, a good yardstick, without barely coming off the bridle. He bolted up in similar fashion in a Group 3 at Goodwood at the end of July and, although not quite as visually impressive, he made his first venture into Group 1 company a winning one when taking the Prix Du Moulin at Longchamp in September. His best performance was reserved for his final start in the Group 1 QEII at Ascot on Champions day, where he halted the winning run of the top-class Palace Pier in a strong renewal. So in just over four months he turned into one of the best horses in training and his 2022 campaign is eagerly awaited. There's enough in his pedigree to suggest he's worth trying over 1m2f but, whichever path connections choose, he is likely to make his mark again at the highest level assuming all remains well. WILLIAM HAGGAS

BAY BRIDGE

4 b c New Bay - Hayyona (Multiplex)

Only the likes of Mick Easterby and Sir Mark Prescott have held a British trainers' licence for longer than Sir Michael Stoute but, although the latter's victories at the highest level have waned in recent seasons, the win of Dream Of Dreams in the 2021 Diamond Jubilee at Royal Ascot shows the veteran can still do the business when he has the right ammunition. Stoute has always excelled when it comes to the development of older horses and, in Bay Bridge, he may have one that can thrust him back into the Group 1 spotlight this year. The unexposed colt had just four runs in 2021 and he won them all, starting with a novice all-weather win at Newcastle, followed by two handicaps at Newbury and York, and he ended his season by beating Majestic Dawn in the Listed Seymour Stakes at Newmarket over 1m2f in October. Everything about him suggests he should be able to take his form to a higher level this time round and it wouldn't be a surprise to see him start off his season in the Group 3 Earl Of Sefton Stakes at Newmarket's Craven meeting – a race his trainer last won with subsequent Juddmonte International/Coral Eclipse winner Notnowcato – before he goes on to try his hand in Group 1 company. SIR MICHAEL STOUTE

BAY OF HONOUR (IRE)

3 b c Shamardal - Kazimiera (Dubawi)

Although handicaps will be more his thing in the short term, Bay Of Honour very much looks the type to keep onside in 2022. Charlie Appleby's colt, the first foal of a Listed-placed 7f juvenile winner, was backed into favouritism and fared better than the bare facts suggest behind the potentially decent Thunder Max (who also figures in these pages) on his debut over 7f at Doncaster in September. Despite losing ground at the start, the son of Shamardal had worked his way into contention inside the last quarter-mile but the exertions of his earlier efforts ultimately took their toll in the closing stages and he faded to finish tenth. However, he was a different proposition on his next start on Polytrack at Kempton, where he bettered his initial Raceform rating to the tune of 20lb when staying on too strongly for subsequent winner Wineglass Bay, the pair pulling clear of a reasonable field that included two other subsequent scorers. Bay Of Honour should have no problem with the step up to 1m, he's open to a fair bit of improvement this year and it would be a surprise if he doesn't add to his tally, either on artificial surfaces or on grass. CHARLIE APPLEBY

BAYSIDE BOY (IRE)

New Bay - Alava (Anabaa)

A 200,000gns yearling, Bayside Boy is a half-brother to, among others, multiple Group-race winner Forest Ranger, and he looked a smart prospect when winning a 7f Newbury novice stakes on debut in July, not requiring the whip to draw clear of Find, who had already shown useful form. He ran another good race over the same C&D a month later but was touched off by the more experienced Masekela in a Listed contest, with that pair pulling clear of the field. He resumed the winning thread in September at Doncaster when getting the better of Reach For The Moon, the winner of his previous two starts, in the Group 2 Champagne Stakes, where he displayed a good attitude in a falsely run race. The third that day, Twilight Jet, boosted the form subsequently by winning the Cornwallis Stakes. Bayside Boy took another step up in grade next time, but he acquitted himself well by finishing a staying-on third behind Native Trail and Dubawi Legend in the Dewhurst Stakes, with that trio well clear of the fourth. He was stepped up to a mile on his final start in the Vertem Futurity Stakes at Doncaster, where he was ultimately outclassed by Luxembourg, but he still ran a race full of promise as he finished third despite meeting some interference 2f out (he would probably have finished a clear second but for that). The 2,000 Guineas will now be his early-season target and at 25-1 he looks a fair each-way bet in that. He should certainly be up to winning at the highest level in due course. ROGER VARIAN

BELLOSA (IRE)
4 b f Awtaad - Poole Belle (Canford Cliffs)

This 30,000 euros yearling from the first crop of 2016 Irish 2,000 Guineas winner Awtaad made an impressive winning debut over 7f at Newmarket in April, despite showing distinct signs of greenness. Her trainer said afterwards, 'I knew Bellosa was good enough to hit the line but she was taking on horses who have run before, so that shows her class. She used the round gallop on the Limekilns for her last piece of work and she was impressive when she went past a good servant of mine, Ambassadorial, and I knew then we had a good one.' She was stepped up to Listed level for her second outing over the same C&D but she took it in her stride to run out a ready winner from a couple of horses with previous winning form. She next stepped up to Group 3 level for the Jersey Stakes but she trailed in a disappointing 14th of 18, although it appears that the soft underfoot conditions were not at all to her liking. Given some time off to recover from that, she was next seen at Kempton in December, this time in a Class 2 handicap over 7f, and she finished a creditable second of eight, albeit well beaten by the winner Edraak. However, she probably raced a bit too close to the pace which left her vulnerable to a finisher, and in any case she's entitled to come on for the run having missed nearly six months of action. Given the impression she made on her first two starts, she looks capable of winning Group races at up to a mile this season and a race like the Atalanta Stakes, which is run at Sandown in August and which the stable won last season with Saffron Beach, may prove right up her street.
JANE CHAPPLE HYAM.

BICKERSTAFFE
4 b c Mayson - Ocean Boulevard (Danehill Dancer)

Owner David Armstrong names all his horses after places in the north-west of England and his Bickerstaffe (a village in West Lancashire) had a productive season with three sprint victories from eight outings in total. By the owner's flagship sire Mayson, the 4-y-o showed he goes well fresh (also won on racecourse debut as a juvenile) when scoring on quick ground at Pontefract in April, but he didn't add to his tally until scoring again at Ascot in July. Things proved tough for him in the Stewards' Cup consolation and in the Ayr Silver Cup (far from disgraced), but he posted his best effort and made it 2-2 at Ascot when winning a competitive handicap there in early October on his final start of the year. He has only had ten career starts so he isn't over-raced by any means for a sprinter, he goes on most ground (unproven on extremes) and, although his rating is close to three figures, he should be able to find a bit more progress this time round. Given his liking for Ascot, it wouldn't be a surprise if he were to return to the track to take his place in the Wokingham at the Royal meeting in June. KARL BURKE

BLACKROD

4 b c Mayson - Hilldale (Exceed And Excel)

Also owned by David Armstrong and also sired by Group 1 winner Mayson, Blackrod, who is named after a town in Greater Manchester, has the potential to develop into a Group-class performer in the forthcoming campaign. Michael Dods, his trainer, knows a thing or two about dealing with classy sprinters and his 4-y-o is bordering on smart after only eight career outings. He stepped up on his reappearance Haydock run (when shaping as though it was needed) in late May when running well at York the following month, and that proved a platform to success as he improved further to win competitive handicaps at Newmarket (6f) and York (5f) before finishing a fine third on his final start in the Ayr Silver Cup behind a pair that raced more towards the far side of the track (he raced more towards the centre) – an effort that can be marked up as it transpired he lost a shoe. He wasn't seen out after that fine effort and he'll race from a 5lb higher mark in future, but there's every reason to think he'll be more than up to the task. He was well beaten on his only start on soft ground but he handles good to soft and good to firm and he is one to look forward to. MICHAEL DODS

BOOMSHALAA

4 b c Shalaa - Summer Collection (Teofilo)

Three wins from five starts and the promise of more to come could be a succinct overview of Boomshalaa's 3-y-o season in 2021. Novice wins at Kempton and Windsor – both over 6f – confirmed him as a potentially smart sprinter, but it was his performance in the Palace Of Holyrood over 5f at Royal Ascot on heavy ground in June that marked him down as a sprinter to follow. Dropped to the minimum trip for the first time that day, he was spotted going strongly when running out of room at a crucial stage inside the last quarter-mile, and he deserves credit for getting as close as he did to Significantly (beaten a head). He would arguably have won that day with a clear passage and he looked interesting back over 6f at Newmarket's July fixture, but he didn't seem entirely happy on the quick ground and faded in the closing stages behind Blackrod, who also figures in these pages. He was only seen once afterwards and he turned in a smart performance to make it 2-2 on AW when comfortably disposing of four rivals at Chelmsford on his final start in September. As that Chelmsford run was only his sixth start, it'll be a big surprise if there's not more to come, and he'll be one to look out for in the big handicaps – though he still has to prove he is fully effective on very quick ground. ROGER VARIAN

BOUNDLESS POWER (IRE)

5 br g Slade Power - Boundless Joy (Montjeu)

If you'd have paused the Virgin Bet Handicap at Doncaster in October with a furlong to run, not many onlookers would have looked beyond Boundless Power as the likely easy winner, so well was he travelling. But, although he responded grittily to pressure, he was unable to shake off the terrier-like Copper Knight and the judge was unable to separate the pair at the line, with the dead-heaters pulling clear of the smart Dakota Gold. Nevertheless, this was still a career-best effort from Mick Appleby's sprinter, who improved to the tune of almost two stones throughout 2021. Although he handles a sound surface, his four wins

last year and all his best form has been on soft or heavy ground and his strong-travelling nature suggests he should be fully effective if returned to artificial surfaces this year. It's likely his upwardly mobile trainer will have a plan – and one that may involve travelling abroad – and he should be able to make his mark from his official BHA rating of 100 or if he's pitched into lesser Group company.
MICHAEL APPLEBY

BROADSPEAR

3 b c Le Havre - Flower Of Life (Galileo)

Despite greenness, Broadspear turned in a useful debut effort to divide Seattle King (fourth in Newbury Listed event next time) and subsequent Leicester nursery winner Already Gone on his debut over 7f on good-to-soft ground at Salisbury in June. He only saw the racecourse once more – at York on much quicker ground almost two months later – but, although he proved disappointing in a traditionally strong maiden, finishing seventh of 16 behind Hoo Ya Mal, the form of that race has worked out really well. This 105,000gns yearling, who is the first foal of a close relation to a 1m6f–2m winner, will be well suited to the step up to middle distances and beyond in the coming season and he should be able to make his mark in novice company before going on to ply his trade in handicaps. It's too early to say he won't be fully effective on fast ground, but he's in good hands and he's sure to make his mark at some point.
ROGER VARIAN

CANDLEFORD (IRE)

4 b g Kingman - Dorcas Lane (Norse Dancer)

For whatever reason, Candleford failed to make the track as a juvenile, but he wasted little time in making up for lost time in his 3-y-o campaign last year and he's the type to make up into a good-quality handicapper this time round. He showed fair form on his first two starts but stepped up appreciably on those efforts to win at Windsor (1m2f) after a break in August. Although disqualified after his rider weighed in 5lb light (his trainer failed to add the weight cloth) at Ascot, next time he still ran a solid race and he progressed steadily over 1m4f on his last three starts – the last two of which came on Polytrack at Kempton. He was put away after winning his final start in the first half of November, but he's the type physically to make further improvement over the winter. He has yet to tackle testing ground, but he seems to go on most other types of terrain and he has the potential to elevate his BHA rating to three figures in the coming months.

WILLIAM HAGGAS

CASH (IRE)

3 gr c Shamardal - Lady Rosamunde (Maria's Mon)

David Simcock had a couple of noteworthy debut juvenile winners in the 2021 season – Light Infantry (also appears in these pages) was a winning newcomer for the yard, and Cash, who won first time up at Newmarket in October, was another that could take much higher ranking this season. His work at home must have been encouraging as he started at single-figure odds in a race where an expensive and choicely bred Godolphin runner headed the market. Despite losing a bit of ground at the start, this 100,000gns yearling, whose price rose to £140,000 as a 2-y-o, made up his ground in the last half-mile and he only had to be pushed out to beat Al Nafir, who franked the form by winning at Kempton on his next start. That was indeed a promising start and, given his pedigree, suggests he should be suited to a step up to middle distances; it will be fascinating to see if he's good enough to go down the Classic route. Something like the Dante at York in May could be an ideal starting point but, whatever path his trainer chooses, he's the type to leave the bare facts of his sole juvenile start a long way behind and he can quickly make his mark in Pattern company.

DAVID SIMCOCK

CATURRA (IRE)

3 b c Mehmas - Shoshoni Wind (Sleeping Indian)

Clive Cox knows a thing or two about training very fast horses having nurtured the careers of Reckless Abandon, Harry Angel and Supremacy, to name but a few – all of whom were able to make their mark at the highest level.

Reckless Abandon and Supremacy both won the Middle Park in their juvenile days, but, while Caturra could only manage fifth behind Richard Fahey's Perfect Power in the most recent renewal of that race, he appeals as the sort who could go on to victory at the highest level this time round. He'll have to raise his game in order to do so, but last year's snug Group 2 Flying Childers winner is a good sort physically and, although he had a busy time of it last year, he's just the type to make progress over the winter and to train on in 2022. Cox said after that Doncaster win: 'Caturra saves his energy for where he needs it. He's got a wonderful mind and a lot of speed. We just had to fine tune how we ride him because he was using too much too early. He's got that quality of a real sprinter in his width of hip and when you stand behind him he's got a serious back end and engine. I'm looking forward to him next year.' It is reasonable to assume he is going to prove most effective on a sound surface and he's likely to be aimed at all the best races over 5f – though that Middle Park run suggests he will be well worth another try over 6f at some point.
CLIVE COX

CLAYMORE (FR)

3 b c New Bay - Brit Wit (High Chaparral)

Jane Chapple-Hyam had a season to remember in 2021 thanks to a breakthrough Group 1 success with Saffron Beach in the Sun Chariot Stakes at Newmarket in early October. Bellosa and Uber Cool both registered three-figure Raceform ratings for the trainer and another one that can be expected to make up into a smart performer this year is Claymore, who created a lasting impression when bolting up on soft ground at Newmarket on debut in the second half of October. This half-brother to a German 1m2f winner only cost £10,000 as a 2-y-o but his value was considerably enhanced when he strode clear in the last quarter-mile to beat market leader Noble Order, who ran to a similar level in defeat at Kempton last time, by 4l. The trainer has reportedly resisted big-money offers from the US, and she said, 'We think Claymore is a Classic horse all right and, all being well, we may run him in the

2,000 Guineas and then the Derby.' Whether he is good enough to get competitive in either of those races is up in the air at present, but what is certain is that he's open to a good deal of improvement and he's sure to win more races. It remains to be seen whether he's as effective on much quicker ground but the early season Derby trials – or the Guineas itself – should prove informative on that score. He should stay middle distances and he's undoubtedly an exciting prospect.
JANE CHAPPLE-HYAM

COROEBUS (IRE)

3 b c Dubawi - First Victory (Teofilo)

Coroebus really should be heading into winter quarters boasting an unbeaten 3-3 record. However, Charlie Appleby's colt was nailed by Mark Johnston's progressive Royal Patronage in the closing stages having been sent on some way out on his second start in the Group 2 Royal Lodge at Newmarket in September. That still represented a big step up on the form he showed in a novice at the July course on his first start – though that debut form worked out tremendously well with runner-up, fourth, fifth and sixth all winning next time. Jockey William Buick held onto him for longer on his third and final start in the Group 3 Autumn Stakes and he posted his best effort to confirm himself as one of the best of his generation, tanking through the race and having too much in hand for Imperial Fighter, who was beaten a similar distance in the Group 1 Vertem Futurity next time. He's the second foal of a half-sister to the owner's dual Dubai World Cup winner Thunder Snow and, although it's not set in stone that he'll stay the 1m4f of the Derby trip, he should prove fully effective at up to 1m2f. He couldn't be in better hands and, with further improvement likely, he should be up to winning races at the highest level at some stage this year. The French Derby, Coral-Eclipse and Juddmonte International, a path almost trod by St Mark's Basilica last year, look like logical targets if it is thought he won't stay 1m4f. CHARLIE APPLEBY

CUMULONIMBUS (IRE)

3 ch c Night Of Thunder - Queen's Novel (King's Best)

A 42,000gns foal out of a 1m3f AW winner, Cumulonimbus caught the eye in the paddock before taking part in a 7f maiden at Doncaster on soft ground in late October. Before the race Charlie Fellowes had said that, 'he is a colt with a bright future. He should love the soft ground and Donny is a lovely place to start horses off at. I doubt he will be winning but he should run well.' Chalked up at 40-1 in the betting, he didn't win but he still ran a pleasing race, finishing third of the 15 runners, keeping on steadily without troubling the more experienced Jimi Hendrix and Beluga Gold, who finished first and second respectively. There was a length back to the fourth, Velazquez, who was having his third start and he would go on to win his next outing off an official rating of 85, so the form doesn't look bad at all. Cumulonimbus has got plenty of size and scope about him and could be pretty useful once tackling middle distances this season. CHARLIE FELLOWES

DARK VEGA (IRE)

3 b f Lope De Vega - Dream Club (Dansili)

This a half-sister to several winners, including Upgraded, Darkened and Dream Point, looked to be the stable's second string behind Paris Lights based on jockey bookings when she made her debut over 7f at the Curragh in October. However, after being a little slowly away, she finished her race off strongly to create a favourable impression on debut at odds of 22-1. She got the better of Boundless Ocean in the closing stages and that horse went on to run two solid races behind Glounthaune and Duke De Sessa in Group 3 races subsequently to give the form a solid enough look. Dark Vega, who was put away after her debut run, looks an exciting prospect for middle distances for the season ahead. She has an Irish Oaks entry and she may well live up to that sort of billing in time. JESSICA HARRINGTON

DEODAR

3 br g Bated Breath - Tested (Selkirk)

Khalid Abdulla had a range of equine champions through his hands in over four decades as an owner – notably Frankel, Dancing Brave, Enable and Arrogate – until his untimely death early in 2021. The Saudi-born owner of Juddmonte Farms has left a lasting legacy in this game and his famous green, white and pink colours are still in evidence. While Deodar has few pretensions to being in the same league as the aforementioned, he's already proved himself to be a smart performer after only two runs and, with similar improvement in 2022, he could easily prove capable of winning in minor Group company. He's from a good Juddmonte family and, although gelded before his debut, he created a good impression to win a Newbury maiden (good to soft) in a race that unearthed several winners last September. He wasn't able to justify favouritism when upped to Listed company at Doncaster on soft the following month, but he turned in an improved performance to chase home a winning machine in Flaming Rib (rated 108) at level weights. He shaped that day as though the step up to 7f would be more to his liking (backed up by his pedigree) and he should be competitive in good-quality handicaps before he tries his hand in a higher grade. RALPH BECKETT

DESERT CROWN

3 b c Nathaniel - Desert Berry (Green Desert)

This son of Nathaniel, who cost 280,000gns as a yearling, is related to four winners, including Flying Thunder, who was a Group 3 (handicap) winner over 7f in Hong Kong. He ran just once towards the end of the year in a Nottingham maiden over 1m, but he was mightily impressive as he put five and a half lengths and more between himself and his rivals, headed by Schmilson, who had previously shown a decent level of form. Never far away, he steadily made his way to the front before finding plenty inside the final furlong to pull right away from his rivals despite running green. His easy win came despite some bad market vibes as he'd drifted to 11-1 in the betting from around 11-2 in

the morning. The same Nottingham maiden was won by Space Blues in 2018 and Mishriff in 2019 and Desert Crown actually recorded a slightly better Raceform rating than that pair, so it looks strong form – it certainly looked a useful effort with a view to a 3-y-o campaign and his breeding suggests that he will stay at least 1m2f.
SIR MICHAEL STOUTE

DISCOVERIES (IRE)

3 b f Mastercraftsman - Alpha Lupi (Rahy)

Jessica Harrington won the Coronation Stakes at Royal Ascot with Alpha Centauri in 2018 and again with Alpine Star in 2020, and she could make it three wins in five years in 2022 with Discoveries, who is a full-sister to the former and a half sister to the latter. Having made a pleasing debut over just shy of 7f at Leopardstown in June, the daughter of Mastercraftsman built on that by getting off the mark at the Curragh over 7f later that same month, despite still showing obvious signs of greenness. She then ran in the Group 2 Debutante Stakes in August, which was named last year in honour of Alpha Centauri, where she ran a solid if unspectacular race as she finished third of eight behind Agartha, beaten around four and a half lengths. She completely turned the form of that race on its head on her final start of the campaign, however, as she put in a much-improved display in the Group 1 Moyglare Stud Stakes in September to get the better of Agartha by three quarters of a length. Alpha Centauri improved dramatically from two to three so there's every chance that Discoveries has more to give and she can already be pencilled in for races like the Coronation Stakes, the Falmouth Stakes and the Matron Stakes, should everything go to plan. She's an exciting prospect. JESSICA HARRINGTON

DRAGON SYMBOL

4 gr c Cable Bay - Arcamist (Arcano)

At the start of 2021 not too many – aside from those connected with him – were familiar with the name Dragon Symbol. However, he finished the year as one of the best sprinters in training and there's the prospect of more to

come now that he's had a little more time to mature. Archie Watson did a tremendous job with him, getting him to win his first four starts, and he confirmed he was a Group-class performer in the Sandy Lane Stakes when nailed in the closing stages (after hanging left) by David Evans' Rohaan, who went on to win the ultra-competitive Wokingham at Royal Ascot. Indeed, Dragon Symbol also did his bit for that Haydock form when passing the post in front in the Group 1 Commonwealth Cup at Royal Ascot, but he was rightly demoted for hanging (again) and causing interference to Campanelle, who was subsequently awarded the race. The son of Cable Bay failed to win again in 2021 but he ran a series of solid races in some of the best sprints until underperforming on Champions Day – where he'd probably had enough for the season – on his final start both of 2021 and for Watson. Unfortunately for the last-named, he switched stables in the latter part of last year and will now continue his development under the watchful eye of Roger Varian at his Carlburg yard. His new trainer said, 'Dragon Symbol joined us before Christmas. He arrived in very good condition and looks fantastic. His form is in the book for everyone to see and he's a very exciting horse for us to look forward to for the season ahead. He's a top-notch sprinter and all the top sprints will be on his radar this year. It's too early to say where we'll start him off just yet and we're just looking forward to getting to know him a bit more.'
ROGER VARIAN

DUBAI HONOUR (IRE)

4 b g Pride Of Dubai - Mondelice (Montjeu)

William Haggas is renowned for improving his horses but even he must have been surprised with the way Dubai Honour progressed throughout 2021. He'd shown himself to be a very useful sort in his juvenile career, but he'd not raced outside of novice and nursery company at two. He made his 2021 reappearance in the Britannia Handicap at the Royal Ascot last June, and, although he fared best of the 14 runners that raced on the far side of the track, that didn't suggest he was going to develop into one of the best mile-and-a-quarter performers in Europe. However, that's how it turned out and he went on a mini winning spree with victory in a traditionally strong Newmarket handicap, followed by a pair of French Group 2 wins at Deauville and Longchamp respectively. His best effort in terms of form, though, came in defeat in the Group 1 Champion Stakes back on these shores in October when he found only Sealiway, who had previously finished a fine fifth in the Arc when not seeming to stay the 1m4f trip, too strong. That prompted his trainer to have a tilt at the Hong Kong Cup on International Day at Sha Tin in December, but he was found out by the tactical nature of that race and he could manage only fourth behind the high-class Loves Only You. Haggas said after the race, 'Dubai Honour ran a really good race and he was just a bit unfortunate with how the race unfolded, which often happens there. When he got out and hit his stride he really came home well. This trip will have taught him a lot and hopefully we'll have a smart international performer on our hands next year.' There's a good chance he'll be heading for the Dubai Turf (1m1f) on World Cup night and he'll be a player in that event, especially if he gets a stronger gallop to aim at. WILLIAM HAGGAS

DUELIST

3 b c Dubawi - Coplow (Manduro)

Duelist won't be the best horse by any stretch of the imagination to grace Richard Hannon's East Everleigh stables, but he's a progressive and unexposed sort who looks just the type to leave his juvenile form well behind in 2022. Hannon knows the family well, having trained his half-sister Billesdon Brook, who left her 2-y-o form a long way behind when causing a 66-1 upset in the 1,000 Guineas in 2018 (also won the following year's Group 1 Sun Chariot). Duelist wasn't seen in public until August, but he showed ability when finishing a respectable fifth at Goodwood in late August in a race that threw up a couple of subsequent winners. He stepped up on that level when fourth behind Cash (also figures in this '100') at Newmarket just over a month later, but he wasn't seen out again and, although he'll be vulnerable against the better types in this grade, he'll be one to keep a close eye on when handicapped, especially

when he's upped to 1m2f. He handles ground on both the easy side and the quick side of good and there's a fair bit of improvement to come this season.
RICHARD HANNON

DUKE DE SESSA (IRE)

3 b c Lope De Vega - Dark Crusader (Cape Cross)

Duke De Sessa, who is a half-brother to 1m2f AW winner Hotspur Harry, caught the eye when finishing third in a 7f Galway maiden last July and he duly delivered on that promise on his second career outing a month later over 1m at the Curragh when winning a decent-looking maiden by four and three quarter lengths. Still quite immature, he took a steep rise in grade next time when he ran in the Group 1 National Stakes over 7f at the same course in September and it all proved a bit much for him as he trailed home sixth of seven finishers behind Native Trail. However, he put his fledgling career firmly back on track a month later as he won the Group 3 Eyrefield Stakes over 1m1f at Leopardstown, where he displayed a decent turn of foot in the closing stages. Dermot Weld said afterwards, 'There is lots to look forward to. Hopefully he can come back early next season for a Guineas trial and I see him as a horse for next year's Irish 2,000 Guineas.' DERMOT WELD

DUTY BOUND

3 b c Kingman - Key Point (Galileo)

This half-brother to 1m4f AW winner Punctuation, who recently opened his duck in a 2m hurdle race for Fergal O'Brien, caught the eye in two 1m maidens at Nottingham in the autumn and he ought to make his mark as a middle-distance handicapper at three on the back of those runs. He finished a well-beaten fourth of eight on the first occasion in mid-October, but the Raceform race-reader commented that the Kingman colt 'shaped promisingly on his debut and should be much sharper for the experience'. That proved to be the case in early November when he finished third of eleven behind odds-on winner Walk Of Stars, improving his Raceform rating by 17lb in the process. However, 1m already looked an inadequate test for him there and he should have no trouble in winning his maiden at around 1m2f in the spring before making his mark over slightly further in handicaps. ANDREW BALDING

EBRO RIVER (IRE)

3 ch c Galileo Gold - Soft Power (Balmont)

Hugo Palmer won the 2,000 Guineas and the St. James's Palace Stakes with Galileo Gold in 2016, but he had to wait another five years before winning his next Group 1 and, fittingly, the horse to do the business for him was Ebro River, a son of Galileo Gold, who won the Phoenix Stakes over 6f at the Curragh in August, a race in which he pretty much made all. That was his seventh start of the season and his rider, Shane Foley, said afterwards, 'He's tough and he's genuine. We just said beforehand that we wouldn't mind changing the tactics a bit. We'd been dropping him in but there didn't look to be much pace today and with that tailwind it can be hard to get them back up front.' They tried the same tactics on his next start in the Group 1 National Stakes over a furlong further but, while he appeared to have many of his rivals in trouble 2f out, he couldn't quite sustain the gallop over the longer trip and he eventually finished a highly respectable third behind Native Trail and Point Lonsdale in what was undoubtedly one of the strongest 2,000 Guineas trials of the year. Ebro River ran once more afterwards, again over 7f, but a line can be drawn through that form as he failed to settle in the Prix Jean-Luc Lagardere at Longchamp in which he ultimately finished eighth of nine on his first start in heavy ground. Rather than step up to 1m like his sire did six years ago, it would seem that a return to 6f will prove ideal and he is one to note for the Commonwealth Cup over that trip at Royal Ascot in June. HUGO PALMER

ELDAR ELDAROV

3 b c Dubawi - All At Sea (Sea The Stars)

Despite clear signs of greenness, this £480,000 breeze-up sales purchase displayed a decent turn of foot on his sole outing in a 1m Nottingham maiden in October to win by 5l from Janoobi, with another 5l back to the third. It was an impressive initial performance and, with his dam a triple Listed winner at around 1m2f, it would seem that a step-up in trip will bring about further improvement at three. Varian confirmed this afterwards: 'He's a horse who has improved as the year has gone on and the family get better with age. He's not been a horse we've been in a rush with. He was ready for his debut and made a very pleasing one. He's one of those horses we'll look forward to next year and see how he winters. I think he will stay at middle distances – 10 furlongs, maybe 12 furlongs. The pedigree would suggest that and the way he galloped out after the line would suggest that too.' He looks a talented individual and, with the promise of plenty more to come, he could make up into a Pattern-level performer before too long. ROGER VARIAN

FILBERT POWER

3 ch c Night Of Thunder - Candleberry (Shamardal)

2021 was Andrew Balding's best year as a trainer since taking over the licence at his Kingsclere base from his Derby and Arc-winning father Ian at the end of 2002. Balding junior bagged 150 wins in 2021 – a personal best – along with win and place prize money of nearly £4.5m on the domestic front. Three-year-olds contributed almost half of those 150 victories and he will likely have another strong team to go to war with this time around. Filbert Power is a horse that should make his mark in novice company before going on to take in the better class handicaps judged on his sole performance in 2021 when second over 6f in soft ground at Doncaster on the final day of the turf season in November. A 175,000gns yearling and a half-brother to a 5f winner, Filbert Power was well found in the market and he showed a useful level of ability by chasing home a similarly promising newcomer in Kidwah, who also figures in these pages. He'll have no problems with at least 7f judged on the way he ran and also on pedigree, and he should come on a fair bit mentally for that first experience of a racecourse. He looks sure to win races. ANDREW BALDING

FIRST OFFICER (IRE)

3 b c Galileo - Weekend Strike (Smart Strike)

Although he disappointed on his AW debut at Kempton in November, First Officer is much better judged on the form of his debut effort at Newmarket in October, where he shaped with conspicuous promise behind the William Haggas-trained Al Mubhir over 7f on good ground. Despite a tardy start, this half-brother to three winners (including 7.4f–1m6f winner Sizzling – including in Group 3 company) made up plenty of ground under fairly considerate handling in the last quarter-mile to finish third, just over 2l behind the winner. That run was franked by next-time out victories of the runner-up, the seventh and the ninth so the form certainly has a solid look to it. Given that initial promise, it's best to give First Officer another chance. It may be that he's just a better horse on turf but, whether that turns out to be the case or not, he'll be worth looking out for in handicaps when he goes over 1m2f and beyond once he's qualified for a mark. He's open to improvement and should win races in his grade.
ROGER VARIAN

FLAMING RIB (IRE)

3 b c Ribchester - Suddenly (Excelebration)

A 16-1 winner of a Nottingham novice stakes over 5f on his second career outing in May, Flaming Rib kept eking out more improvement throughout the season, eventually adding another four wins to his CV, with all four of those coming under Pierre-Louis Jamin, who is still unbeaten on the colt. The winning spree started in a Thirsk nursery in July, when Flaming Rib was rated 92, and it culminated in a Listed win at Doncaster in October, when he was rated 108. All of the victories came over 6f and they were all gained in similar fashion as he either raced very prominently or made all. He's a son of Ribchester, who excelled at 1m, and there is also stamina on the dam's side of the family, so it could be that he can make further progress as he steps up to 7f or 1m as a three-year-old. Michael Owen recently ended his relationship with trainer

Tom Dascombe at Manor House Stables in Cheshire and Hugo Palmer now looks the likely replacement. He has many exciting horses to look forward to, including this fellow. HUGO PALMER

FLYIN' SOLO

5 br g Roderic O'Connor - Fille Good (Cape Cross)

David Menuisier has made quite a name for himself in recent years through the exploits of Thundering Blue, Danceteria, Migration and the ill-fated but highly talented Wonderful Tonight. Flyin' Solo has some improving to do before he can be mentioned in the same bracket as that quartet, but he's just the type to progress further in 2022 as he matures and he appeals as the sort that could win a good-quality handicap at around 1m4f. Unraced as a juvenile, he didn't see the track until late in his 3-y-o career but he improved to the tune of about a stone on turf last year. Handicap wins at Newbury (1m2f) and York (just shy of 1m4f) confirmed him to be a useful performer and he turned in his best effort in defeat back at Newbury in July. Gelded after that outing, he didn't see the racecourse again until the final day of the turf season and he ran respectably to finish seventh of 23 in the November Handicap on his first start in soft ground – despite not quite seeing the race out as well as the principals. He may be suited by a less testing surface and, given that he's only had five runs on turf (and nine starts in total), it wouldn't surprise to see him making up into a smart performer this time round. DAVID MENUISIER

FOXES TALES (IRE)

4 b c Zoffany - Starfish (Galileo)

A combination of the step up to Group 1 company and the fitting of blinkers resulted in Foxes Tales turning in a disappointing effort in the Champion Stakes on his final start in October (he finished seventh of nine behind Sealiway). Up to that point he had been a steadily progressive sort in 2021 and he's well worth another try at the highest level this year. But, back to the beginning. Following an eye-catching AW run on his sole juvenile

start, the 400,000gns yearling wasn't seen to best effect in the Listed Dee Stakes at Chester on his reappearance, but he showed a fair chunk of improvement to win on his handicap debut in a more truly run Golden Gates Stakes (1m2f) at Royal Ascot in June. Better was to come as he was narrowly touched off in a strong Newmarket handicap (just beaten by another '100' inclusion Dubai Honour, the pair clear) and he opened his account in Pattern company when landing a Group 3 at Haydock in August. He matched that in a similar event at Newbury the following month, where he was touched off by the progressive Solid Stone, before bombing out in the headgear when returned to Ascot. He should be stronger and more mature with another winter on his proverbial back and he's one to look forward to in 2022. He seems to handle most ground with the exception of extremes and he is effective from 1m2f–1m3f.
ANDREW BALDING

FRESH

5 b g Bated Breath – Kendal Mint (Kyllachy)

Fresh comes with an element of risk attached, especially as he bled from the nose and returned with an irregular heartbeat after his final start over 7f on soft ground at Doncaster, but there's little doubt that he's capable of picking up a good-quality handicap back over 6f at some point this year, assuming he's back to full health. His turf season started in good fashion when he picked up an Ascot handicap over 6f on good-to-soft ground in May and he turned in a career-best effort when just touched off by Rohaan in the Wokingham Stakes over the same C&D the following month. Conditions (soft) looked to be in his favour for the Stewards' Cup at the end of July, but he could only manage eighth of 24 following a tardy start and after racing away from the main action. The return to 7f and another trip to Ascot didn't bring about any improvement after a two-month break in early October and, although he shaped more encouragingly at Doncaster on his penultimate start, finishing third of ten behind Magical Spirit, he was well beaten on that final outing. A strongly run 6f with give in the ground looks to be his requirements and he could

easily be a late-maturing type who finds his best form as a 5-y-o. His style of racing means he needs things to slot perfectly into place, but he's well worth another chance.
JAMES FANSHAWE

GIRL ON FILM (FR)

3 b f Dabirism - Pretty Paper (Medaglia D'Oro)

Ralph Beckett, who has held a training licence for over 20 years, has a good record with fillies down the years. Among others, he has won the Oaks twice with Look Here and Talent and, in 2015, his Simple Verse became the first filly since User Friendly in 1992 to win the St Leger. A debut victory for Girl On Film at Newmarket (July course) in August certainly wasn't unexpected as she started as 7-4 favourite for a maiden fillies' event and she justified that support in comfortable fashion by coming clear in the closing stages to beat Bellstreet Bridie. She switched to the Rowley Mile and was upped a fair way in grade to Listed company for her only other start of 2021 and, although she lost her unbeaten record, she shaped with a fair bit of promise after getting a bit unbalanced in the dip when fifth behind Hello You. She was just behind subsequent impressive scorer Jumbly that day and, with the first three also showing the form was solid, she has a good platform to build on for this season. Her pedigree suggests she should stay 1m2f and, so far, she's only raced on a sound surface. She's capable of better. RALPH BECKETT

GLOUNTHAUNE (IRE)

3 b c Kodiac - Khaimah (Nayef)

A disappointing run in the Breeders' Cup Juvenile Turf was a rather sour note on which to end the year for this big son of Kodiac, but he had shown enough ability in his three runs before that to be forgiven that one poor effort as he embarks on his 3-y-o career. He edged out Castle Star, the winner of his next two starts, on his debut in a 6f Curragh maiden in April and he was then not seen again until October when reappearing in the Group 1 Dewhurst Stakes where he finished, on the face of it, a rather modest sixth of eight behind Native Trail. However, he caught the eye of the Raceform race-reader who said that Glounthaune 'is the one in behind to take from this, as he was keeping on when lacking a clear run over 1f out. He would have been closer at the end and can definitely come on for this big-race experience.' Sure enough, just a week later he won the Group 3 Killavullan Stakes over 7f at Leopardstown and his rider Seamie Heffernan was full of praise for him afterwards: 'He's a horse with a huge future. I've been a little bit disappointed with a few of ours lately and I think if this lad was himself he'd have gone around there on the bridle. But, in fairness, he showed a great will to win.' He's got plenty of untapped potential at three and he could well end up in something like the French Guineas early on in the season. AIDAN O'BRIEN

GO BEARS GO (IRE)

3 b c Kodi Bear - In Dubai (Giant's Causeway)

After he won the Group 2 Railway Stakes over 6f at the Curragh on just his third career start in June, Go Bears Go's trainer David Loughnane was ecstatic: 'I absolutely adore him. I said from the start that he was the best I've trained. It took some bottle for the owners to stump up ten grand to supplement him. They reaped the reward. It's lovely when a horse proves you right. I think we will come back for the Phoenix Stakes.' Go Bears Go did indeed run in that Group 1 over the same C&D about six weeks later, finishing a gallant third behind Ebro River and Dr Zempf. He was again not disgraced when finishing fourth behind Perfect Power on his next start in the Group 1 Middle Park Stakes in September, while he appeared to not quite stay 7f when finishing seventh in the Dewhurst. Perhaps for that reason the Juvenile Turf Sprint (5f) was chosen as his race at the Breeders' Cup rather than the Juvenile Turf (1m) and he ran a cracker as he finished second, splitting two Wesley Ward-trained runners, Twilight Gleaming and Kaufymaker. That was only half the story though as he was uncharacteristically slow away from the gates and that almost certainly made the difference between finishing first and second. Loughnane said, 'I said five furlongs might be too sharp for Go Bears Go and in another five yards he wins.' Nevertheless, it proved that sprinting may be his game at three and races like the

Commonwealth Cup over 6f at Royal Ascot will surely come under consideration for him now. DAVID LOUGHNANE

GOLDEN LYRA (IRE)

3 ch f Lope De Vega - Sea The Sun (Sea The Stars)

Everything about Golden Lyra's pedigree smacks of middle distances and she looks a generous price at around 33-1 for those who like an ante-post dabble for the Epsom Oaks on the first Friday in June. Throw into the mix that she is trained by one of the best in the business in William Haggas and the fact that she created a really favourable impression at Newmarket on debut and Golden Lyra is a name that could be a familiar one by the end of the season. This half-sister to dual 1m4f winner Going Gone went off as third-favourite behind market leaders trained by John & Thady Gosden and Charlie Appleby in the first division of a fillies' novice over 7f in October, but she proved much too good for her rivals, powering clear inside the last quarter-mile to win by upwards of 5l. That marked her down as one who would be able to hold her own in stronger company and it'll be interesting to see whether she goes down the Guineas route or whether she's campaigned with a middle-distance career in mind. If it is the latter, a race like the Musidora at York's Dante meeting could be a good starting point – a race that the stable won in 2018 with Give And Take. Whichever path she treads, though, she's a potentially Group-class performer whose reappearance is eagerly awaited. WILLIAM HAGGAS

GREAT AMBASSADOR

5 ch g Exceed And Excel - Snoqualmie Girl (Montjeu)

Luca Cumani's former assistant Ed Walker had his first taste of Group 1 success last summer when Starman proved too good for Dragon Symbol in the Darley July Cup. However, that one was retired to stud before he really had time to fill his imposing frame and Great Ambassador – rated only 8lb behind him on Raceform ratings – may be the one to take his place in Group company this time round. He hasn't had too much racing for a sprinter, but he showed he's on the verge of Group class with some solid efforts in the best sprint handicaps throughout the year. He'd have gone even closer to winning the Stewards' Cup at Goodwood in August had he not veered from the far side into the centre of the track in the closing stages on the rain-soaked ground. Wins at Newmarket (July course) and York soon followed, but he turned in a personal best when chasing home the enigmatic Bielsa from a mark of 106 in the ultra-competitive Ayr Gold Cup on his final start in September. Following that race his trainer said, 'What's sad is that Great Ambassador could have had the most incredible handicap season. The plan was Wokingham, Stewards' Cup and then here but there was the ground at Ascot, the draw and the ground at Goodwood and the draw today. It's so frustrating and he's a proper horse.' Expect him to be on the mark sooner rather than later in 2022. ED WALKER

HAFIT (IRE)

3 b c Dubawi - Cushion (Galileo)

Hafit only recouped around £20,000 of his yearling price of 2,100,000gns during his first racing season, but he improved with every outing and he looks the sort to make his mark in Group company at some point in 2022. That price tag, coupled with his pedigree and, no doubt, his homework, saw him go off at a shade of odds-on for his debut at Newmarket (July course) in August, where he showed plenty of ability and a gritty attitude to beat Razzle Dazzle in a race that threw up numerous winners. Although stepping up on that level in terms of form, he didn't look overly happy on the quick ground at Haydock in a Listed event next time and he was beaten by Kevin Ryan's Triple Time at skinny odds. However, he reserved his best effort for his final start in the 1m2f Group 3 Zetland Stakes, where he seemed to relish the extra yardage and he was only narrowly denied by stable companion Goldspur and Joseph O'Brien's Unconquerable – who finished third and fifth respectively in the Group 1 Criterium de Saint-Cloud next time. The son of Dubawi is bred to improve again this year over a distance of ground, and he could even make up into a credible St Leger contender come the autumn. He's in a yard that is chock full of 3-y-o talent, but it'll be a surprise if he doesn't end the season a Group winner. CHARLIE APPLEBY

HEAT OF THE MOMENT
3 ch f Bobby's Kitten - Heat Of The Night (Lear Fan)

This half-sister to some fair winners including Here To Eternity, who is the dam of two Group 1 winners in Hong Kong, was an unconsidered 33-1 shot when she made her debut in a 6f Yarmouth novice stakes in mid-October but she showed plenty of ability and a good, straightforward attitude to run out a two and a half length winner from the 81-rated Favourite Child. The runner-up went on to boost the form subsequently by finishing a head second in a 5f Listed race at Longchamp, in which she recorded a Raceform rating of 97. Owner-breeder Kirsten Rausing said afterwards that Heat Of The Moment would be spending the winter at her stud before being aimed at the French 1,000 Guineas in the spring. The filly is the first Rausing-owned runner to be handled by Jane Chapple Hyam and the trainer may have hit the jackpot on her first attempt. JANE CHAPPLE-HYAM

HEBRIDES (IRE)
3 ch c Mehmas - Woodland Maiden (Mastercraftsman)

A 105,000gns breeze-up purchase by Highclere in April, Hebrides finished a promising third in 6.5f Newbury maiden in October on heavy ground, making a nice move from off the pace after a sluggish start, which he couldn't quite sustain late on. He looked a lot more streetwise on his second outing at Doncaster on the final day of the Flat turf season, winning a 6f event with the minimum fuss. He is an athletic-looking colt out of an unraced mare, Woodland Maiden, whose sister Iveagh Gardens was a Group 3 winner in Ireland over 7f at three. It will be over that sort of trip that Hebrides should excel as a three-year-old and he looks a smashing prospect for the season ahead.
WILLIAM HAGGAS

HELLO YOU (IRE)
3 b f Invincible Spirit - Lucrece (Pivotal)

Out of a half-sister to Group 1 winner Signs of Blessing, Hello You ran out an impressive winner over 6f at Wolverhampton on her debut in May, quickening up well in the straight and drawing clear without her rider having to go for his whip. She next ran in the Group 3 Albany Stakes at Royal Ascot in June, where she finished an excellent second to Sandrine and she was third behind the same horse a month later at Newmarket in the Group 2 Duchess Of Cambridge Stakes. Switched from Ralph Beckett after that run to the up-and-coming yard of David Loughnane, she posted a couple of underwhelming efforts for her new trainer in the Lowther Stakes at York and the Prestige Stakes at Goodwood, but she looked a different horse at Newmarket in September as she ran out a convincing winner of the Group 2 Rockfel Stakes over 7f. That was a career best and she ran another good race in the Breeders' Cup Juvenile Fillies Turf at Santa Anita, where she finished fifth behind Pizza Bianca, a race in which she was a shade keen just in behind the speed and as a result she just failed to see it out. That was her first attempt at 1m and she looks well worth another chance at that sort of trip as a 3-y-o. She has an entry in the Irish 1,000 Guineas and she would certainly deserve her place in the line-up. Based on her Rockfel form, she looks capable of adding further Group races to her CV as she matures. Speaking in January, Rossa Ryan picked her out as the horse he is most looking forward to in 2022, saying: 'I think she's a proper filly. Ascot got to her too soon, we were never to know that and the next two or three runs I spent just trying to get her to relax and it all fell right back again in the Rockfel. She looks a million dollars and she's filled out into that lovely fine mare that we all thought she would be.' DAVID LOUGHNANE

HERMANA ESTRELLA (IRE)

3 b f Starspangledbanner - The Last Sister (Lord Shanakill)

It's slightly worrying that Hermana Estrella hasn't been seen since May, having run only once as a juvenile, so admittedly she's a slightly risky entry to the hundred. However, she is in because of the impression she left on that one start in a Group 3 at Naas over 6f. She was the 50-1 outsider of a field of seven but, despite looking raw and running green, she ran out a convincing winner, reeling in the Gavin Cromwell-trained Quick Suzy in the closing stages to win with her ears pricked. The runner-up franked the form in no uncertain terms next time out as she bolted up in the Queen Mary Stakes at Royal Ascot, beating Twilight Gleaming, who herself would go on to win the Breeders' Cup Juvenile Turf Sprint at the end of the year. Hermana Estrella's rider Chris Hayes said after her win, 'She's a very smart filly and Fozzy [Stack] doesn't make entries like that unless they are good.' The win was achieved on soft ground and it remains to be seen whether that will be essential to her chances in the future. She has an entry in the Irish 1,000 Guineas in May and hopefully we will see her in a trial for that race in the spring. FOZZY STACK

HURRICANE IVOR (IRE)

5 b g Ivawood - Quickstep Queen (Royal Applause)

Having joined William Haggas from France in May, Hurricane Ivor improved in leaps and bounds throughout the season and there are more Group races to be won with him on quick ground at five. Having toiled on soft ground over 5f at York on his first start for the yard in late May, he quickly found his groove at Sandown over the same trip on his next start in July, dead-heating with Phoenix Star in controversial circumstances (he looked the winner but the mirror used in the photo finish was incorrectly aligned). The trainer said afterwards, 'He ran poorly first time but had been training much better since and this was a little bit lower grade. He needed every yard here, and a flat six or a stiff five will be his game. I thought the ground might be too soft for him today, but it wasn't.' He was unlucky again next time as won the race on his side of the track over 5f at Ascot, only to be beaten a short head by Significantly, who had raced on the other side – the next four home all raced on the same side as the winner. He ran no race in the Stewards' Cup three weeks later, but that was on soft ground which clearly doesn't suit him and he bounced back to form at York next time when a close third in a top 5f handicap. He improved again next time by winning the Portland Handicap at Doncaster in September off top weight and that form was boosted subsequently by the runner-up Boundless Power, who won his next two starts. Hurricane Ivor had now climbed to a mark of 107, which meant he was upped in grade and he took it in his stride as he saw off Moss Gill, Tis Marvellous and his old adversary Significantly in a Group 3 over 5f at Newbury. His final start of the season at Ascot can be ignored as it was again run on ground that didn't suit him. That brought his record on ground officially described as soft for Haggas to 008, while his record on good to soft or faster reads 12311. Still on the up, he can add to his Group race tally in 2022 provided he has the right underfoot conditions. WILLIAM HAGGAS

JOHN LEEPER (IRE)

4 b c Frankel - Snow Fairy (Intikhab)

Ed Dunlop's impeccably bred John Leeper, who is by superstar Frankel out of a multiple Group 1-winning mare, ultimately proved disappointing in 2021 after his season promised so much early on. Only raced once as a juvenile, the colt, who is named after his trainer's late father John, hit the ground running early in his 3-y-o career when bolting up in a decent-looking Newcastle novice event over 1m2f in April. Despite a tendency to pull hard, he followed up in Listed company at Newmarket in May over the same trip, in the process showing a fine attitude to beat a reliable yardstick in Tasman Bay, with the pair clear of Fancy Man, who did his bit for the form by finishing a close second in a Group 3 at Haydock next time. The turning point in John Leeper's season may have been when he ran in the Derby in which he was a big disappointment, again racing with the choke out and failing to handle the undulations, beaten before the longer 1m4f trip should have been an issue. He failed to add to his tally in four subsequent starts, but he at least ran respectably on each occasion, including on his final outing in November at Kempton when tried in cheekpieces, where he finished eighth, although not beaten far. Given his strapping physique, the best of him almost certainly is to come, and it's to be hoped he has matured and learnt to settle over the winter. In the hope that he is not pitched straight into the best company early next season, there are races to be won with him in Listed or minor Group company. A strongly run 1m2f may suit him best in the short term and he's yet to race on ground more testing than good to soft. ED DUNLOP

JUMBLY

3 b f Gleneagles - Thistle Bird (Selkirk)

The winner of three of her four races over 6–7f at two, this daughter of Gleneagles out of a 1m2f Group 1 winner should be able to win again as she steps up in trip at three. She made a winning debut in a 6f Leicester maiden in July and that race worked out well subsequently with the third and fourth winning next time out. Jumbly herself went on to win a four-runner Kempton novice over 7f in early September by three and three quarter lengths and the runner-up won next time out so the form of that race looks solid too. She tasted defeat on her next outing in the Group 2 Rockfel Stakes at Newmarket, but she came from a lot further back than the three fillies who finished in front of her and so her effort can be upgraded as it clearly was a race in which it paid to race handily. The following month she posted a career best at Newbury, again over 7f, as she won a Listed race by four and three quarter lengths from a host of previous winners. That was on soft ground and it may well be that a bit of cut will bring the best out of her as she resumes her career. She could end up in the 1,000 Guineas in May for the new father–son training partnership, but it is perhaps over slightly further that she will prove most effective. HARRY & ROGER CHARLTON

KIDWAH (IRE)

3 b f Kodiac - Areeda (Refuse To Bend)

It's an accepted fact in racing circles that horses based with William Haggas improve a fair bit for their debut runs (something that is backed up by the stats). So, when he has a winning newcomer it's reasonable to assume that they could probably turn out to be well above average. That could definitely be the case with Kidwah, who looked potentially smart when beating Filbert Power (another one of the '100') first-time up at Doncaster on the final day of the turf season in November. Despite a tardy start and a tendency to run green, this 220,000gns foal and half-sister to 5f–7f (including Group 3 winner) Great Page created a favourable impression to account for the Andrew Balding runner, with a subsequent winner (trio clear of the rest) back in third. She should have no problems with 7f on that evidence and she is sure to come on for the run. At this stage it isn't clear whether she won because of the soft ground or in spite of it but, whatever her underfoot preferences turn out to be, she looks the type who should be able to hold her own in stronger company in 2022. WILLIAM HAGGAS

KING OF THE CASTLE (IRE)

4 ch c Galileo - Remember When (Danehill Dancer)

A full brother to 2020 Epsom Derby winner Serpentine, King Of The Castle was steadily progressive as a 3-y-o in 2021 and, with further improvement to come as he steps up in trip, he could easily become a decent Cup horse for team Ballydoyle in 2022. Sent off favourite for a 1m2f maiden at Leopardstown in April, he finished a modest fourth behind Southern Lights, but he fared a little better on his next start over 1m4f at the same course in May, finishing third of 18 behind The Mediterranean, having tried to nick the race from the front. He was perhaps a little unlucky in the Ulster Derby over half a furlong further at Down Royal the following month as he lost his place 2f out before running on strongly to finish second behind Iowa, but he finally came good at Limerick in July, winning an ordinary maiden over 1m4f 110y by over 4l. He looked like he might already benefit from a step up in trip at that stage and he was duly sent to York to contest the Melrose Handicap over 1m6f in August, where he finished a good sixth of 22 behind Valley Forge. He was unlucky not to finish a little closer, however, as he missed the break and was then forced to race wide, but he showed a good attitude as he kept plugging on all the way to the finish. He saved his best run till last though as he finished an excellent fourth of 13 behind Sonnyboyliston in the Group 1 Irish St Leger over 1m6f at the Curragh in September, despite only bringing an official rating of 95 into the race. He was nearest at the finish which augurs well for him as he steps up to 2m and beyond at four. He'd have to improve a fair bit to make it to the Ascot Gold Cup in June, but it wouldn't be the biggest shock to see him line up in that race should everything go to plan in the interim. AIDAN O'BRIEN

KORKER (IRE)

3 b g Dandy Man - Adaptation (Spectrum)

There are Listed or Group sprints to be won this year with this son of Dandy Man, who made a good impression in his juvenile season, winning three times and finishing second twice in eight starts. A big eyecatcher when narrowly touched off by Project Dante at 25-1 on his debut at York in May, he duly got off the mark at Carlisle later that month despite wandering across the track in the closing stages. He was pitched into the Group 2 Norfolk Stakes after that but it came a bit too soon for him and he finished in midfield after a tardy start. However, the following month he won an ordinary Thirsk novice stakes over the minimum trip by 5l to quickly get back on track. He then finished a fair seventh of 20 in a valuable sales race over 6f at York in August, where he raced too freely and he was again far too keen when finishing down the field in the Group 2 Flying Childers Stakes at Doncaster in September. Dropped into calmer waters again, he won a Haydock nursery off 88 in September and he almost followed up at York the following month off a 4lb higher mark but, having looked the most likely winner, he lugged right in the closing stages to lose out narrowly to Josies Kid, with that pair 3l clear of the rest. That puts him on a mark of 95 for the new season, but the fact that he's already contested a couple of Group 2s suggests his connections consider him better than a handicapper, so you have to think he remains fairly treated. Surely it won't be too long before he can take Listed or Group honours.
KARL BURKE

LADIES CHURCH

3 ch f Churchill - Rioticism (Rio De La Plata)

Twice a winner over 5f in the summer, including a Listed race at Naas which she won by two and a quarter lengths, Ladies Church gave the impression in two subsequent outings that she would appreciate a step up in trip as she gains further experience. She ran a perfectly good race behind a pair of Ger Lyons-trained runners in a Group 3 over 6f at the Curragh in August, but she couldn't quite go the initial pace before making some decent late gains and it was a similar story in a 5f Listed contest at Dundalk in early October, where she was again noted as doing her best work in the closing stages. Her dam was a 5f winner in France but she's by Churchill and it may be that trips of around 7f or 1m may prove best for her at three. She has no fancy entries but it seems likely that she can make her mark at Group level in due course. JOHNNY MURTAGH

LIGHT INFANTRY (FR)

3 ch c Fast Company - Lights On Me (Kyllachy)

With a bit more improvement to come, Light Infantry could easily turn into a credible outsider for the 2,000 Guineas at Newmarket in May. At the time of writing, his odds range from 25-1 to 33-1 and he's certainly created a good impression so far, winning on his debut at Yarmouth and following up in a Listed event at Newbury. Word was obviously out ahead of his debut run (over 6f on fast ground) at the seaside venue in the middle of September and he started as 3-1 second-favourite in a field of eight headed by market leader Ideal Guest, who had shown progressive form in three previous starts. Although the last-named disappointed that day, there was no mistaking the promise shown by Light Infantry, who pulled clear in the closing stages to beat fellow newcomer High Velocity by over 6l and the latter did his bit for the form by winning at Wolverhampton on his next start. David Simcock's juvenile had an altogether different test for this next start at Newbury – the 7f Horris Hill Stakes, which was staged on very different ground (soft) – but he was equal to the task despite hanging badly right in the conditions, to beat a competitive field comprising a stack of previous winners. That should have brought him on mentally and he is the type on looks to improve physically over the winter. He could head back to Newbury for the Greenham – run over the same trip as the Horris Hill – before going up again in grade. He is bred to stay 1m and he is an exciting prospect. DAVID SIMCOCK

LIONEL
3 ch c Lope De Vega - Gretchen (Galileo)

The Normandie Stud is a significant operation that has bred (and owned) Group 1 winners such as Fallen For You, Duncan and Sultanina, along with a stack of other high-profile winners. And the stud looks to have another potentially smart sort in Lionel, who shaped with a good deal of promise on his only start when second in a Newbury maiden on heavy ground at the end of October. This second foal of a Listed/Group 2 winner – herself a half-sister to the aforementioned Duncan – made a big move on the outside before throwing down a challenge on that debut run, but he was just run out of it by the more experienced Zain Nights, with the pair pulling a couple of lengths clear of the remainder. While that bare form is nothing out of the ordinary, he should have no problems winning a similar event in the coming season before going on to better things. If his pedigree is anything to go by, he'll be very well suited by a step up to middle distances and beyond, and we are likely to be hearing a fair bit more about him in the coming months. DAVID MENUISIER

LONG TRADITION (IRE)
5 b g Shamardal - Irish History (Dubawi)

In terms of what he has achieved on a racecourse, Long Tradition wouldn't be anywhere near the best horse to be housed in the Newmarket yard of Saeed Bin Suroor. However, he's included in this list as an unexposed sort who could land a decent handicap this year. Despite only having a Chelmsford novice win to his name, he was rather pitched into the deep end in the competitive Cambridgeshire for his handicap debut and he ran respectably (in first-time cheekpieces) on the quick ground that day to finish eighth, one place ahead of subsequent winner Naval Commander. He bettered that effort on his final start of 2021 when chasing home Roger Charlton's One Journey at a respectable distance over 1m2f on soft ground at Newbury (also in cheekpieces) in late October. He'll have to raise his game if he's to win one of these in 2022, but there's every chance

that he has some improvement in him and, if things do go to plan, races like the Hunt Cup, the John Smith's Cup – a race his trainer has yet to win – and another tilt at the Cambridgeshire, could be on the cards.
SAEED BIN SUROOR

LOVE TROPHY POWER

3 ch f Bated Breath – Desire (Kyllachy)

After this daughter of Bated Breath finished third of eight in a 6f Yarmouth fillies' novice stakes behind Majd in mid-September, the Raceform race-reader described her as 'a likeable stamp of a filly who gave the impression that she won't be too long in winning something similar before going on to better things at up to 1m.' Two weeks later she ran in another fillies' novice over the same trip at Kempton and, on the face of it, it was perhaps a little disappointing that she couldn't quite get her head in front, having looked all over the winner (touched 1.05 on the Betfair exchange close to home before getting caught after drifting to the right). However, the filly that narrowly beat her, Sky Blue Pink, went on to boost the form by winning another novice at Haydock under a 6lb penalty two weeks later and that pair had pulled over 2l clear of the third at Kempton. Love Trophy Power, who wasn't seen again, should have no trouble winning a similar race in the early part of the season, after which she can then make her mark in handicaps at up to a mile. She is very much one to keep onside.
ROGER VARIAN

LUSAIL (IRE)

3 b c Mehmas - Diaminda (Diamond Green)

Having won two of his first three races in the early part of the season, a maiden at York which worked out well and a novice stakes at Newmarket which also produced a host of subsequent winners, Lusail emulated his sire Mehmas by winning the Group 2 July Stakes at Newmarket in the height of summer. He was game as he held off two horses who finished strongly and his rider Pat Dobbs said afterwards, 'It was close for comfort but he's got a brilliant attitude and is laid-back. The faster the ground the better for him.' With Goodwood run mainly on soft or heavy ground last season, Lusail skipped the Richmond Stakes and he was instead sent to York where he defied a 3lb penalty for his earlier Group 2 win by taking the Gimcrack Stakes with a minimum of fuss. His trainer Richard Hannon said afterwards: 'This is the one two-year-old who really has the class and the scope for next year. He's undoubtedly a Guineas horse. He's in the Middle Park, Dewhurst and the Lagardere and he'll take one of those on.' However, he skipped all those engagements, presumably because of the ground, and instead he ran in the Champagne Stakes at Doncaster, which was a four-runner affair on good-to-soft ground at Doncaster in September. He trailed in last of the quartet but it is probably best to draw a line through that form as it was a falsely run race on ground which clearly didn't suit. Look out for him in truly run races on quick ground – if it comes up fast for the 2,000 Guineas he could be a threat to all and his current odds of 40-1 (50-1 in a place) would certainly underestimate him.

RICHARD HANNON

LUXEMBOURG (IRE)

3 b c Camelot - Attire (Danehill Dancer)

Luxembourg went into winter quarters as the clear Derby favourite on the back of a campaign that saw him remain unbeaten in his three starts, culminating with victory in the Group 1 Vertem Futurity Stakes at Doncaster in October. The son of Camelot, who cost 150,000gns as a yearling and is a half-brother to three winners from 7f–1m4f, got his season off to the perfect start when beating a previous scorer Tuwaiq at Killarney in July and he won with such authority that he was pitched into the Group 2 Beresford Stakes over 1m on his second outing in September. Despite still showing signs of greenness, he was far too good for Manu Et Corde, with the aforementioned Tuwaiq back in third spot. Softer ground was a potential pitfall at Doncaster – as was the steady gallop – but he overcame both in workmanlike fashion to notch his first win at the highest level. While the bare facts of that contest are nothing out of the ordinary (for a race of that standing) he'd have been much better suited by a stronger gallop and he's in pole position now to emulate his sire Camelot, who landed the English Guineas/Derby double ten years ago. Since 2012 his trainer has won the Guineas a further four times and the Epsom Derby another five times. After the Doncaster race O'Brien said, 'Luxembourg would have preferred a stronger gallop, he's a big high cruiser and he got there a little bit after halfway. He was very babyish in front but he's a lovely horse. You'd have to be delighted with him really. The lads will decide but what he's able to do over four furlongs at home says that he probably wouldn't have any problems starting in the Guineas if that's what they wanted to do. Hopefully he will be something to look forward to.' He should have no problems staying the Derby trip and, given his physique, there should be a fair bit of improvement in him in 2022. AIDAN O'BRIEN

MAGICAL SPIRIT (IRE)

6 ch g Zebedee - La Dame De Fer (Mr Greeley)

In each of his four seasons racing, Magical Spirit has notched a win in either September or October. And, given that he was better than ever last year and that his trainer has a penchant for winning the Ayr Gold Cup, it's a fair bet that his season will be geared towards winning that showpiece event this autumn. Although he has gone well fresh before (won on reappearance in 2020), he was below his best until a fine third in the Shergar Cup Sprint at Ascot in the first half of August, his fourth outing of the year. He then headed to Ayr – this time for the Silver Cup – and finished a highly creditable fourth, but he went on to post personal bests at Doncaster in October and November. On the first occasion he relished the soft ground and had far too much in hand of Music Society, eventually winning by two and a quarter lengths, and he raised the bar even higher on his final start when he was just touched off by King's Lynn over the same course and distance in the Listed Wentworth Stakes. Those improved efforts, both over 6f, mean he should be weighted highly enough to ensure his place in the Ayr Gold Cup this time around (even should he drop a pound or two in the meantime) and he's a name to keep in mind for the second half of the season, especially when the ground starts to ease. KEVIN RYAN

MAJESTIC GLORY
3 b f Frankel - Bella Nouf (Dansili)

A daughter of Frankel and a half-sister to a 1m2f winner, Majestic Glory caught the eye in two maidens in July, both over 6f, in which she finished sixth and second. She delivered on that early promise by easily winning a 6f novice stakes at Newmarket at the end of the same month and just one week later she landed the Group 3 Sweet Solera Stakes over 7f at the same course. At that stage she looked a highly progressive filly, with David Probert saying, 'It was a quick turnaround for Majestic Glory but we know she handles this track very well. She's got a great attitude. She got slightly boxed in on the inside but she's nimble enough to find her way out of trouble and hit the rising ground well. She's progressing quite nicely.' However, the wheels came off afterwards as she was never remotely in contention in the Rockfel Stakes in September after missing the break and she trailed in a disappointing last of nine in the Fillies' Mile on her final start in October. While those two runs will set alarm bells ringing, it's just possible that she may have felt the effects of those initial four runs within the space of a month in the summer and she should be given another chance to show her true colours at three. Her sights will no doubt be lowered slightly in the early part of the season but she's still in the Irish 1,000 Guineas and hopefully she can bounce back to that sort of level in due course.
ANDREW BALDING

MEHNAH
4 b f Frankel - Asheerah (Shamardal)

This Frankel half-sister to Kevin Prendergast's Irish 2,000 Guineas winner Awtaad looks sure to win Group races at four provided she stays fit and healthy – the fact that she has only raced three times in two seasons tells you that, unfortunately, she has been hard to train so far. An impressive winner of a Dundalk maiden in September 2020 which worked out well, she returned to action in April in the 1,000 Guineas Trial at Leopardstown over 7f. She finished second in that, beaten a head, but she was the one to take out of the race. She raced well off the pace, was green and she still had plenty of work to do turning in, but she gradually picked up and was really motoring at the finish to lose out only narrowly to Keeper Of Time. Unfortunately, she was forced to miss the Irish Guineas but we saw her again in July when she won a Listed contest over 1m at Killarney despite very little going right for her in the race. She was slowly away and she was parked wide all the way up the straight and received a bump or two as well, but she quickened up inside the last furlong and was always going to get there. Her rider Chris Hayes said afterwards, 'Mehnah had an awkward niggly injury just before the Irish 1,000 Guineas and it has been baby steps with her. She was very undercooked but fit enough for that level and I have no doubt that she is a Group 1 filly.' However, she returned from that race 'a little stiff' and, while plans were made for her to race again in September, those were ultimately shelved. She's not one to abandon lightly, however, and assuming she returns fit and well, she should soon be making up for lost time. KEVIN PRENDERGAST

MIGRATION (IRE)

6 b g Alhebayeb - Caribbean Ace (Red Clubs)

Forced off the track by injury for nearly two years from September 2019 to June 2021, Migration showed that he had lost none of his ability by winning two of his four starts last season and there could be more to come from him as a 6-y-o in 2022. He returned from 641 days off at Salisbury in late June, running a race full of promise as he finished a close fourth to Johan over 1m after running on strongly in the closing stages, having been stopped in his run at a crucial stage of the race. He backed up that initial promise by running away with a good handicap at Glorious Goodwood over 1m2f the following month, having briefly looked in trouble 2f out, and he defied an 8lb higher mark at York in August as he touched off Sinjaari in the closing stages having again met some trouble in running. His trainer commented afterwards: 'Migration has come back from injury and he's special. He's in the Cambridgeshire but he'll have a lot of weight so I'm not sure about that.' He ultimately skipped that competitive handicap and instead took part in a Listed race over 1m2f back at Goodwood in September, but he was reportedly unsuited by the drying ground that day as he dropped away to finish last of seven finishers. Forgive him that effort and watch out for him in Pattern races at up to 1m4f this season – he looks sure to win again. DAVID MENUISIER

MO'ASSESS (IRE)

4 ch c Pivotal - Hush Money (Hussonet)

Saeed Bin Suroor has rather been put in the shade in recent times by fellow Godolphin trainer Charlie Appleby. However, the Dubaian has in no way lost his touch and he showed what he could do when getting the right type with his handling of Real World, who went from Royal Hunt Cup winner to Group 2 winner in the space of about three and a half months. Bin Suroor also landed the Cambridgeshire with Bedouin's Story in 2021 and he has another interesting type for that race in Mo'assess this time round. Following a promising debut run at Nottingham (1m, good) he was afforded an easy lead and won convincingly on his next two starts – both over 1m on Polytrack at Kempton. Although he didn't add to his tally when returned to turf, he showed enough over 1m2f at Newbury (didn't fail through lack of stamina) or when dropped back to 7f on soft at Doncaster on his final start to suggest he'll be of interest in similar company in the coming months. He should prove fully effective from 1m to 1m2f and, given he's only had the five racecourse starts, he should be able to take his official BHA rating into three digits at some point this year.
SAEED BIN SUROOR

MOJO STAR (IRE)

4 b c Sea The Stars - Galley (Zamindar)

Following two runs at Newbury – one in October 2020 and one in a maiden (1m2f) on reappearance last May – the logical view was that Mojo Star would have no problem winning a maiden or a novice before going on to prove himself as a 100+ horse. However, the strapping son of Sea The Stars took a monumental leap forward in terms of form when finishing second behind Adayar at 50-1 in the Epsom Derby (one place ahead of subsequent Irish Derby and English St Leger winner Hurricane Lane). Trainer Richard Hannon stated after the race: 'Mojo Star has always been the most gorgeous horse we've had at our place for a long time. He travelled like a really good horse but he didn't handle the undulations.' Many considered the Epsom run to be a bit of a fluke, especially when he could manage no better than fifth in the Irish Derby but, after a bloodless win at cramped odds over 1m4f at Newbury in August, he showed himself to be a high-class performer by chasing home strong stayer Hurricane Run in the St Leger. A trip to Longchamp for an Arc staged on heavy ground proved a bridge too far at the end of a fairly tough campaign in October (he finished tenth of 14) but he reportedly stays in training. Rossa Ryan, the owner's retained rider, said after that run: 'I travelled super into the straight. This lad over 1m4f just seems to always lack half a gear, but you don't want to light him up and make too much use of him. I think Mojo Star is going to be a top horse at two miles next year.' It is hard to disagree with that assertion, especially given his run over 1m6f in the St Leger and given that there could be more in the way of physical improvement to come. Whether he stays the Ascot Gold Cup trip of 2m4f is another matter, but he can make his mark from 1m6f to 2m this year. RICHARD HANNON

MOSTAHDAF (IRE)

4 br c Frankel - Handassa (Dubawi)

Mostahdaf's only venture into Group 1 company last year resulted in a heavy defeat, but the bare form only tells half the story of his run in the St James's Palace Stakes at Royal Ascot. He went there boasting a perfect 3-3 record, having looked a useful sort at Newcastle (7f) on debut before going on to land a conditions event at Kempton (1m), and he improved again when notching his third win in the Listed Heron event (soft) at Kempton on his turf debut in May. So, it was all systems go for Royal Ascot but, just as he was starting to mount a challenge early in the home straight,

he was badly hampered and he was unable to recover, eventually allowed to come home in his own time by Jim Crowley, some 17l or so behind Jim Bolger's winner Poetic Flare. He was given three months off before being seen again in the Fortune Stakes – also over 1m at Sandown and also on soft ground – and he confirmed himself an improved performer by getting back to winning ways, in the process accounting for top handicappers Escobar and Sir Busker. His best effort was reserved for his final start at Newmarket where he accounted for Cambridgeshire winner Bedouin's Story and previous Yarmouth scorer Finest Sound in comfortable fashion. That run, over 1m1f, showed he didn't need a soft surface in order to show his best form. Joint trainer John Gosden, who has had a plethora of top-class horses through his hands down the years, said, 'Mostahdaf hasn't done a lot wrong. He got boxed in during the St James's Palace Stakes and that was the end of it. We've always thought of him as a 1m2f horse. His half-sister [Nazeef] won two Group 1 races at a mile. She was by Invincible Spirit and he is by Frankel so we are pretty confident a mile and a quarter is his best trip. I was going to leave him in the Champion Stakes but I got overruled by the management and that is why he is here today. He would go on good to firm and good to soft he just wouldn't want it firm. He is a classy horse who is probably a next year horse.' There will be plenty of options for him from 1m to 1m2f and he could easily end up developing into a Coral Eclipse/ Juddmonte International type later in the season.
JOHN & THADY GOSDEN

MUJTABA

4 b g Dubawi - Majmu (Redoute's Choice)

An official rating of 98 still looks pretty generous for this unbeaten son of Dubawi out of a South African Grade 1 winner and he should be able to win a decent handicap at around 1m2f before establishing himself as a Graded performer at four. Mujtaba made his debut in an uncompetitive 1m maiden at Chepstow in August and he could do no more than win that by four and a quarter lengths from a subsequent winner, with another 11l back

to the third. That was on good-to-soft ground, but he showed that he handled faster conditions just as well when comfortably landing the odds in a Chester novice over 7f 127y in September. He was given a handicap mark of 90 after that win and he exploited it in October at Redcar, when comfortably seeing off Empirestateofmind, the winner of three of his previous four races, in a 1m event. He was put up 8lb for that win but, as the Raceform race-reader observed, 'Mujtaba looked streets ahead of his opening mark as he maintained his unbeaten record in uncomplicated fashion, in control after taking it up going strongly over 2f out.' Trips of around 1m2f will suit the gelding ideally on breeding and he looks sure to pick up a decent handicap or two before going onto bigger and better things.
WILLIAM HAGGAS

NATASHA

3 ch f Frankel - Darkova (Maria's Mon)

If Natasha turns out to be anywhere near as good as her illustrious half-brother and triple Group 1 winner Almanzor, then she should have a productive time of things this year. She's clearly highly regarded and she was progressing steadily until floundering in the Prix Marcel Boussac – France's premier race for juvenile fillies – on Arc day in early October. Though she had a bit to find strictly on form for that event, she looked worth her place in the line-up given that she had won novice events at Kempton and Sandown on her second and third starts respectively, with that turf run on good ground looking an especially useful piece of form. However, conditions at Longchamp were almost swamp-like and she floundered in the heavy ground – eventually finishing last of the eight runners. She has a long way to go before she can be mentioned in the same bracket as the yard's leading 1,000 Guineas/Oaks candidate Inspiral, but she is in very good hands and she is well worth another chance. The filly should be able to bag an early-season Listed race before going on to hold her own in minor Pattern company. She should stay at least 1m2f and she handles Polytrack and good ground. JOHN & THADY GOSDEN

NATIVE TRAIL

3 b c Oasis Dream - Needleleaf (Observatory)

At this stage of his career, Charlie Appleby's Native Trail has a fairly similar profile to Pinatubo, his champion 2-y-o of 2019, in that he finished his juvenile career unbeaten and bagged two Group 1 events in the Vincent O'Brien Stakes at the Curragh and the Dewhurst at Newmarket in the second half of the season. The trainer will be hoping Native Trail is able to build on his debut season, whereas Pinatubo, who did win a Group 1 at Deauville as a 3-y-o, was never able to match the form he showed in that scintillating 9l win in the Vincent O'Brien. Native Trail started at odds-on for his debut at Sandown and showed he was an above average type by beating Royal Patronage – who went on to success at Group 3 and 2 level – by 4l. He was quickly moved into Pattern company after that and scraped home by a short head from subsequent Listed winner Masekela in the Group 2 Superlative Stakes at Newmarket's July meeting. The step up to Group 1 company was the next step and he posted a much-improved effort to beat Aidan O'Brien's hitherto-unbeaten Point Lonsdale by a ready three and a half lengths. The Dewhurst was the next logical step and, once again, he confirmed he was just about the best of his generation when staying on too stoutly for Dubawi Legend. After that race his trainer said, 'I think we have got a fantastic horse on our hands for next year's 2,000 Guineas. On the back of Coroebus as well we are in a very fortunate position to be going into the winter with two fantastic colts. Native Trail came in at 540kgs from the breeze-ups and full credit to the team who purchased him and Norman Williamson who consigned him. Once he met the rising ground, there was one thing he wasn't going to do and that was stop galloping. I can't see him going any further than a 1m personally but I like to be proven wrong. He is a horse that will go into the winter as an exciting Guineas horse.' As his trainer said, he should have no problems staying 1m and his physique strongly suggests he should train on and be even better this year. He's one to look forward to.
CHARLIE APPLEBY

NEW LONDON (IRE)

3 b c Dubawi - Bright Beacon (Manduro)

At a top-priced 50-1, New London looks worth a small each-way dabble in the Epsom Derby ante-post market. Although he only won by a neck at Newmarket in October – his only juvenile start of the year – there is little doubt he should prove considerably better than those bare facts and he appeals as a Group-winner in the making. This brother to 7f Listed winner Al Dabaran was helped by the late defection of stable companion Al Nafir but, after missing the break, he made up a good deal of ground under mainly hands and heels riding in the last quarter-mile or so before getting up in the closing stages to nail useful maiden Soul Stopper, prompting his trainer to say, 'New London is German bred and we knew he'd enjoy the ground and the trip. He'll make a nice middle distance horse next year.' There could be a degree of understatement in that line and, although he'll have to raise his game by a considerable amount if he is to be considered either a live Derby or St Leger prospect, he is in very good hands with Appleby, a trainer who has won two of the last four Epsom Derbies and also the most recent running of the St Leger. He'll have no problems staying at least 1m4f and, although that run came on soft ground, there's no reason to think he won't be as effective on a sounder surface and he's a really interesting prospect.
CHARLIE APPLEBY

NOBLE TRUTH (FR)

3 b c Kingman - Speralita (Frankel)

A headstrong individual at two, there's plenty more to come from Noble Truth as he matures mentally, and he already has a few pieces of form which suggest that he should be winning Group races in due course. A promising third behind subsequent July Stakes winner Lusail on his debut in June, he got off the mark on his second outing at Newmarket a month later, winning a 7f novice stakes, with four of the next six home winning next time out. Noble Truth himself ran disappointingly in the Group 3 Acomb Stakes next time over 7f at York, with his tendency to pull hard proving his undoing, but he came good again over the same trip at Doncaster in September as he won a Listed race despite again taking a keen hold early on. Alex Merriam, Charlie Appleby's assistant, said after that run: 'It's nice to get Noble Truth back on track. He won nicely at Newmarket and disappointed last time for no apparent reason. He settled better today and I'm pleased with him. I just had a quick chat with Charlie and there are no immediate plans but we'll stick to seven furlongs.' He did indeed run over that trip next time in the Prix Jean-Luc Lagardere at Longchamp and he ran a fantastic race, only losing out close to home to another promising sort, Angel Bleu, with that pair pulling clear of Ancient Rome in third. His trainer had predicted before the race that 'he's a strong galloper who can maintain it,' and he was certainly proved right about that, plus his charge clearly handled the heavy conditions at Longchamp. He ran nowhere near that level on his final start at Newbury, again over 7f, but on that occasion he simply pulled far too hard which cost him any chance as he weakened to finish a modest fourth of seven in a Group 3 contest. However, his two runs before that marked him out as a future Group winner and he can only improve as he learns to settle better in his races. CHARLIE APPLEBY

OCEAN WAVE
4 ch f Le Havre - Gold Sands (Cape Cross)

The first foal out of a Listed-placed AW winner (1m–1m4f; Raceform rating 95), Ocean Wave made a promising debut behind the William Haggas-trained Belief in a 1m Thirsk fillies' novice stakes in June, prompting the Raceform race-reader to say that she 'finished her race off in notably taking fashion, once the penny had dropped with her, and a success in something similar should be a formality before hopefully going on to better things.' She perhaps didn't progress as much as expected the following month at Haydock in a similar contest over the same trip, but she still finished a fair third behind Mobadra and in hindsight it may not have been enough of a test of stamina for her. She took a big step up in trip next time on the all-weather surface at Lingfield as she tackled a 1m4f maiden, but she was ridden confidently, travelled much the best and only a tendency to lug right in the home straight prevented her from winning with even more authority. She was awarded an official mark of 79 after that and she made light of it over 1m2f at the same course in early September, winning a fillies' handicap by 5l, with the runner-up, Lower Street, franking the form by winning four of her next five starts. Ocean Wave was put up to 86 for that easy win but that still looks very workable as she resumes her career. JAMES TATE

PEARL GLORY (IRE)

3 b f Cotai Glory - Oatmeal (Dalakhani)

Kevin Philippart De Foy is a French-speaking Belgian who learned his trade under the tutelage of Criquette Head in France, John Oxx in Ireland and Christophe Clement in the US. The 30-year-old is now based in Newmarket and is quickly establishing himself as a talented up-and-coming young trainer, with 30 winners coming from his yard in 2021. Pearl Glory, a £12,000 breeze-up purchase in June 2020, has a pedigree that's a mix of speed and stamina and she showed plenty of ability for her young trainer in her juvenile season which she can hopefully build on at three. She won a five-runner novice over 6f at Lingfield in July, with the second and fourth both winning next time out to give the form a solid look. She then went on to win a Salisbury novice stakes over the same trip in August, where she touched off an odds-on shot, the Organiser, with that pair pulling nearly 7l clear of the rest. Two weeks later she contested the Group 3 Dick Poole Fillies' Stakes over the same C&D for new owners and she acquitted herself well as she finished second of 12 runners behind Romantic Time. She was stepped up to 7f for her final start of the season, another Group 3, this time the Oh So Sharp Stakes at Newmarket, but things didn't quite go to plan for her. She dwelt in the stalls, was playing catch-up throughout and, while she did keep on well inside the final furlong, she was never really in contention as she finished sixth of the nine runners. She deserves a chance to atone for that defeat and she can surely make her mark at around 1m as a three-year-old. KEVIN PHILIPPART DE FOY

PEARL PALINKA (IRE)
3 b f No Nay Never - Catch The Eye (Oratorio)

A full sister to Listed 6f winner Servalan, Pearl Palinka made a good impression in a 5f Tipperary maiden at the end of June, finishing third of eight behind subsequent Listed winner Ladies Church, who had the benefit of previous experience. She was made co-favourite for a hot maiden over 5f 164y at Navan two months later, but she did too much in the early part of the race and finished sixth of the 14 runners, leaving the Raceform race analyst in no doubt that she was far better than the result implied. Six of the first eight home all went on to win next time so it was an exceptionally good maiden in any case, and Pearl Palinka did her job nicely at Down Royal just one week later as she ran out a comfortable winner of a 5f event, with the race-reader saying, 'the manner in which she quickened up inside the last furlong to go and win her race was quite taking. She could go an extra furlong and perhaps she could be smart enough for a stakes race.' Oisin Orr, who rode her to victory, was equally impressed: 'Pearl Palinka had excuses at Navan, she was a bit fresh and got a bit tired, but she has progressed and hopefully she can keep going. I think she will.' She wasn't seen again afterwards but she is a decent prospect for Listed or Group sprints as a three-year-old.
DERMOT WELD

PERFECT NEWS
3 b f Frankel - Besharah (Kodiac)

Besharah was a Group-class filly for William Haggas a few years ago and her daughter Perfect News, who is by Frankel, looks to have inherited plenty of her dam's ability. She finished a good second in a strong-looking Yarmouth maiden over 6f in early August and she built on that two weeks later when getting off the mark over the same trip at Carlisle. She wasn't beaten too far in the Group 3 Dick Poole Fillies' Stakes (6f) on her third outing in early September, but she raced a tad keenly and also hung left which didn't help her cause at all. Dropped into a nursery off her opening mark of 93 next time, she kept on strongly in a 7f contest at Newmarket to edge out Eidikos, with the pair well clear of the third. She was put up 7lb for that to a mark of 100 so it was decided to pitch her into Group company again, this time in the Group 3 Oh So Sharp Stakes, again over 7f at Newmarket. She moved into a promising position in that contest from about 2f out only to get outpaced by the principals, but she still finished a respectable third behind Fast Attack and Allayaali. She already gave the impression there that she will appreciate stepping up to 1m and she can make her mark in Group races over that sort of trip in due course. WILLIAM HAGGAS

POINT LONSDALE (IRE)

3 b c Australia - Sweepstake (Acclamation)

When Point Lonsdale won the Group 2 Futurity Stakes at the Curragh in August by four and a quarter lengths to make it four wins from four runs, the Raceform race-reader noted: 'He looks to be the best two year old around until something else can lay a convincing claim to the contrary.' Well, a very strong claim duly came from the Charlie Appleby-trained Native Trail just one month later as he cleared away from Point Lonsdale in the National Stakes over the same C&D to win by three and a half lengths. This time the race-reader said about Point Lonsdale: 'Only time will tell whether this was his true running or not, but the turbo didn't kick in from the 2f pole like it had done in the Tyros and Futurity.' He wasn't seen again afterwards while Native Trail upheld the form by winning the Dewhurst in similarly impressive fashion and he now rightly heads the market for the 2,000 Guineas. However, Point Lonsdale is still reportedly regarded as Ballydoyle's main hope of winning that Classic (ahead of Luxembourg) and the vibes coming out of the yard are that he won't finish behind Native Trail should they meet again. If that is the case, odds of 12-1 at the time of writing for the 2,000 Guineas look tempting, especially when you consider that Native Trail is just 3-1. It remains to be seen whether the bullishness from within the team will prove to be justified but one defeat does not mean he's suddenly a bad horse and he can surely win his share of races at three. AIDAN O'BRIEN

PURPLEPAY (FR)

3 b f Zarak - Piedra (Lawman)

Having shown a modicum of ability in a maiden and two conditions races in the summer, Purplepay found a new level of form once encountering softer ground in the autumn. She did what was required of her in winning an ordinary 1m1f conditions race at Vichy on soft ground in September, but she markedly stepped up on that when winning a valuable event at Longchamp over 1m on very soft ground in early October. Three weeks later she took part in the Group 1 Criterium International over the same trip at Saint-Cloud, which was also run on ground described as very soft, and she ran well to finish on the heels of Angel Bleu and Ancient Rome, having been denied a clear run about one and half furlongs out. Granted similar conditions, she should continue to find further progress, especially as she steps up in trip. She may well emerge as an interesting contender for the Prix De Diane, which is run over ten and a half furlongs at Chantilly in June and, failing that, there should be a few prizes to be won with her over similar distances in autumn when the mud is flying. CEDRIC ROSSI

RAVENS ARK

5 ch g Raven's Pass - Wonderful Desert (Green Desert)

The winner of two races over 1m4f in 2021, this son of Raven's Pass should be capable of adding to that tally as he steps up to around 2m at five. He was consistent in the early part of the season, winning once and placing twice in four starts over 1m4f from April to June before being stepped up to 1m6f at Sandown in July. He ran a great race there, keeping on well in the closing stages to finish a close-up third behind Dancing Harry and the first five home all went on to win again next time, so the form looks rock-solid. Ravens Ark's own win came back over 1m4f at Brighton, which was also the scene of his other win last term, but he was stepped back up to 1m6f on his final two starts of the season in August. Firstly, he finished sixth of 12 at Sandown but he ran much better than that result implies as he was well back turning for home before getting no run in the straight and, by the time he finally got going having been switched to the outside, it was all too late. He then ran a fine second behind the progressive Snowalot, another of the hundred, over the same trip at Goodwood, where he was a bit short of room 2f out before staying on well in the closing stages. That run suggested that a step up to 2m is imminent and, still only rated 80, there should definitely be more races to be won with him over his new trip. It seems that he will be kept away from soft turf, however, as all of his best form has come on quicker ground. HUGHIE MORRISON

SACRED BRIDGE
3 b f Bated Breath - Sacred Shield (Beat Hollow)

Gradually progressive in her first four starts between June and August, Sacred Bridge remained unbeaten in those four runs and her Raceform rating improved from 85 to 97, then to 101 and finally 110 as she won the Group 3 Round Tower Stakes over 6f at the Curragh by nearly 4l. She showed plenty of speed, travelled comfortably at the head of the gallop and, when asked to quicken, she really lengthened and drew clear in not much more than a few strides. It looked certain that there would be more to come from her and she was duly sent off the 13-8 favourite for the Group 1 Cheveley Park Stakes at Newmarket in late September. She ran no sort of race, however, weakening 1f out to finish a well-beaten eighth of 12 runners behind Tenebrism. The fact that she raced away from the main action may not have been ideal but it certainly wasn't the reason for her below-par display. She deserves a chance to atone for that as she resumes her career, however, with Shane Lyons, Ger's assistant, saying after her Curragh win: 'She's an absolute diamond and she's the sort of horse that you get up in the morning for. Colin [Keane] was very impressed with her. We'll worry about getting a trip next year.' Perhaps she will be kept to 6f or 7f initially, but she's got an Irish 1,000 Guineas entry and if she recovers her spark quickly she may well take up that engagement. GER LYONS

SAGA

3 gr c Invincible Spirit – Emily Bronte (Machiavellian)

An official mark of 92 should be one that John and Thady Gosden can exploit with Saga in 2022 as he looks to have plenty of scope for further progress based on the three runs he had as a juvenile. Owned by the Queen, he was uneasy in the betting on his debut over 7f at Newmarket in July, but he ran a race full of promise, finishing second to Charlie Appleby's Modern Games, who had the benefit of previous experience. Saga bumped into another Appleby-trained improver on his next outing over a mile at the same course a few weeks later, but he made Coroebus pull out all the stops before weakening near the finish. The first six home in that novice stakes went on to win races subsequently so the form looks rock-sold. Saga himself got off the mark in an Ascot maiden over 7f in early September, where he comfortably saw off Koy Koy, who went on to win his next start by six and a half lengths. The grey is a brother to 6f–7f winner Lockwood (including a Group 3; Raceform rating 116) and a half-brother to Earnshaw (1m 2-y-o including a Group 3; 113), so it will be interesting to see what trip he is tried over next. It would appear likely that he will start off at around 1m and then the Gosdens will take it from there. He can certainly make up into a Pattern-class performer.

JOHN & THADY GOSDEN

SAMOOT (IRE)

4 ch f Dubawi - Muthabara (Red Ransom)

Sir Michael Stoute should be able to take advantage of a handicap mark of 89 with this filly in the coming season after she had a satisfactory 3-y-o campaign in 2021. She started her season off with a couple of wins – a 7f novice stakes at Wolverhampton in April and a handicap off her opening mark of 80 at Salisbury in May. She was then a beaten favourite off 86 at Wolverhampton later the same month but she had excuses for that reverse (a wide trip/got going too late) and she bounced back to form when second of 21 runners behind decisive winner Create Belief in the Sandringham handicap at Royal Ascot in June, in which she finished clear of the rest. Her final start of the season was a shade disappointing on the face of it as she finished fifth of 11 in a fillies' handicap over 7f at Newmarket in July but she wasn't given a hard time once her chance had gone (she lost two places close home) and she appeared not to be suited by the slightly faster underfoot conditions. She's no superstar but she should win handicaps off her current mark at around 1m with a bit of cut and she remains one to be interested in. SIR MICHAEL STOUTE

SCOPE (IRE)

4 ch c Teofilo - Look So (Efisio)

It was noted earlier in these pages that Ralph Beckett is a bit of a dab hand with his middle-distance fillies. He's not too shabby when it comes to dealing with the boys either and his Scope made a considerable amount of improvement throughout the season to end up as a Group 1 winner. Following his first two runs of 2021 – a close second in a Newmarket novice in April and when a respectable third in the Lingfield Derby Trial in May – he looked a smart sort who might be able to make his mark in lesser Group company but, although far from disgraced, he had his limitations exposed in the Great Voltigeur Stakes over 1m4f at York's Ebor meeting in August and in the St Leger the following month. However, the son of Teofilo raised his game on his next start when beating a strong field in a Listed event at Ascot (1m6f) in early October and he turned in a personal best when bagging that Group 1 Prix Royal-Oak (French St Leger) over a trip just shy of 2m at Longchamp on his final start later in the month, in the process giving jockey Rob Hornby his first win at the highest level. As that was only his seventh start, there's probably further progress to come this year and, although his stamina for the Ascot Gold Cup trip of 2m4f would have to be taken on trust, he's unexposed over 2m and he should be able to add to his tally – either at home or abroad – in the coming months. RALPH BECKETT

SISSOKO (IRE)

3 b c Australia - Love Excelling (Polish Precedent)

It didn't take former Irish Champion Jockey Donnacha O'Brien long to make his mark at the highest level in his new career as trainer. In his first full season as a licence holder in 2020, his Fancy Blue notched the Group 1 French Oaks and she followed up in the same grade the same month (July) by taking the Nassau Stakes at Goodwood. O'Brien also showed that he was capable of mixing it at the top table on home soil by taking the Group 1 Moyglare Stakes at the Curragh with Shale that autumn. Although O'Brien didn't reproduce the Group 1 success last season, the young trainer had 11 horses that achieved a Raceform rating of 100 or more and he could break back into the big time in 2022 with Sissoko. This half-brother to Dan Excel – a Group 1 winner in Hong Kong and Singapore – stepped up a fair way on the form of his debut effort at the Curragh in September when bolting up over 1m1f when returned to that track on his second start a month later. And, although upped markedly in grade for his third and final run of 2021 in the Group 1 Vertem Futurity Stakes at Doncaster, the colt showed he wasn't far off the best of his generation with a fine second to Luxembourg. His effort probably needs marking up given the steady gallop wouldn't really have been to his liking (he's essentially a resolute galloper). Wayne Lordan, his rider, said after the Doncaster race, 'Donnacha always thought he was a very nice colt. Sissoko won his maiden a week and a bit ago. He was going to make a huge step up to this race, but he looked like he could run a big race and Donnacha was duly right. He's a very straightforward colt and he stays very well. He feels like he's going to be a better three-year-old. He tries very hard and he gets the mile really well which suggests he's going to stay further next year and he feels like a colt that could strengthen up over the winter as well. It was a very good run going into the winter with prospects of next year.' He's likely to be given a Derby preparation rather than a Guineas one and either the Ballysax or Derrinstown will be pencilled in first before a tilt at either the Epsom or Irish Derby. DONNACHA O'BRIEN

SOMETHING ENTICING (IRE)

4 b f Fascinating Rock - La Chapelle (Holy Roman Emperor)

David Elsworth, who called time on his illustrious training career at the end of 2021, will be fondly remembered for horses like Persian Punch, Desert Orchid, Oh So Risky, In The Groove and Arabian Queen, to name but a few. One of the better performers for him in his final season (and the final winner trained by him) was Something Enticing, who won three races in 2021 and who rounded off her season by finishing a close second of 18 to Vesela in a 1m2f Listed race for fillies at Doncaster on the final day of the turf season. She started the year on an official rating of 67 and ended it on 95, which shows how far she came, but there's every chance that she can eke out further progress and establish herself as a Pattern-level filly in 2022. She's mainly been kept to ground with a bit of cut so far and her best trip appears to be around 1m2f so look out for races which fit the bill. They might include contests like the Nottinghamshire Oaks in late April or the Rothesay Stakes at Ayr in May, which will no doubt be pencilled in for her in the early part of the season by Andrew Balding, who was confirmed as her new trainer in January.

ANDREW BALDING

SNOWALOT (IRE)

5 b g Camelot - Bright Snow (Gulch)

Newmarket-based trainer James Ferguson, who served his apprenticeship with Sir Mark Prescott and Jessica Harrington, hasn't taken long to create a good impression in the training ranks, aided in no small way by wins of Zoetic (Listed) in 2020 – his first full season with a licence – and he hit the big time when El Bodegon bagged the Group 1 Criterium de Saint-Cloud last October. His 25 domestic winners in 2021 were gained at a 14 per cent strike-rate and yielded total earnings of almost £300,000. Snowalot contributed two wins to that tally and, although he didn't seem to last home over 2m2f on his final start in the ultra-competitive Cesarewitch at Newmarket in October, he's the type to take his form to a higher level in the coming season. He improved to the tune of just over a stone last year, with both his wins coming over 1m6f, one on quick ground and the other on good to soft, and he didn't fail through lack of stamina when upped to 2m at Haydock in September. That Cesarewitch run was only his ninth start and, although he'll need to improve this year in order to make the cut, a race like the Ebor at York in August could be a realistic target. It'll be a surprise if he doesn't add to his tally in 2022. JAMES FERGUSON

STAR OF INDIA (IRE)

3 b c Galileo - Shermeen (Desert Style)

This brother to 2-y-o winner Roman Empire (subsequently renamed SJ Tourbillon), who finished second behind Mohaafeth in last season's Group 3 Hampton Court Stakes at Royal Ascot before being shipped off to Hong Kong, was fairly impressive when making a winning debut in a 7f maiden at Leopardstown in late October. He was off the bridle almost the whole way as they went a decent gallop and it took until the final furlong for the penny to drop with him. When it did, he really lengthened and he ultimately scored by a comfortable two and a quarter lengths from Sir Antonino, who brought a decent level of form into the race. Seamie Heffernan said afterwards, 'Star Of India is a grand staying type. We went a good gallop and I stayed going well. I like him.' He will come into his own over middle distances this season and, once he learns how to race properly, he could be genuinely exciting. AIDAN O'BRIEN

STONE AGE (IRE)

3 b c Galileo - Bonanza Creek (Anabaa)

It has been a while since Aidan O'Brien notched the most recent of his four wins in the Group 1 Criterium de Saint-Cloud, but he often runs a decent type in the race (one-time Derby favourite Bolshoi Ballet finished fifth in the 2020 renewal) and he has a decent staying type on his hands in Stone Age, who finished second in the latest one. He is arguably one of the best maidens in training given his official rating of 109, though he's likely to go straight for a recognised Derby trial in Ireland rather than gain a bloodless victory against fellow non-winners. Following two promising efforts in maidens at Leopardstown and Galway respectively, he showed that he could compete in Group company when second to Atomic Jones over 1m in a Group 2 back at the first-named track in September. The drop back to 7f wasn't ideal in the Prix Jean-Luc Lagadere at Longchamp on Arc day (he finished sixth in that) but he turned in his best effort when upped to 1m2f in the Criterium, making relentless progress in the last quarter-mile to get within striking distance of El Bodegon on very soft ground. Whether he will be quick enough for a fast-ground Epsom or Irish Derby is open to debate but, although he would be an interesting outsider should the ground come up testing in either of those races. The principal aim for him this season could be the English St Leger at Doncaster, a race his trainer has already taken on five occasions this century. AIDAN O'BRIEN

SUNRAY MAJOR

5 b c Dubawi - Zenda (Zamindar)

A lightly raced colt with a fine pedigree/strike-rate and housed in the stable of one of the best yards in the country: all the ingredients you need – assuming he stays sound – to ensure that Sunray Major can win a good handicap or a minor Group event in the coming months. This half-brother to the top-class Kingman was off the course for just over 450 days on the back of a 3-y-o campaign in 2020 that yielded a debut novice win from only two runs. However, he looked an improved performer on his comeback in September 2021 when winning over 7f at Chelmsford on his first AW start. Even better was to follow as he made short work of a decent field on his handicap debut over 7f at Ascot in October and, given his progressive profile, he went off as a 2-1 shot for a traditionally well-contested handicap return to 1m back at the Berkshire venue on Champions Day two weeks later. For whatever reason (it could have been the result of three fairly quick runs in succession) he wasn't at his best and he faded in the closing stages to finish 14th of the 20 runners.

He'll be well worth another chance over 1m – it wasn't necessarily the trip that beat him – and he could be just the type to make an impression in a race like the Lincoln at Doncaster at the end of March, a race the Gosdens won last year with a similar type in Haqeeqy. He's evidently a well-regarded type and let's hope he stays sound in 2022. JOHN & THADY GOSDEN

TATSUMAKI
3 ch c Charming Thought - Kasumi (Inchinor)

The form of Sales races is sometimes suspect but anyone who saw Tatsumaki's demolition job in the Tattersalls October Stakes at Newmarket (6f) in autumn could have been in no doubt that they'd just seen a potentially top-class animal at work. He had already looked a useful sort when winning both his starts at Newmarket (7f, July course) on debut in August and when dropped to 6f on Tapeta at Newcastle the following month. However, he took his form to a new level on the Rowley Mile course, returning to Newmarket in early October when thrashing the 104-rated Fearby (who admittedly wasn't at his very best) by 5l. After the race trainer Marco Botti said, 'We came into the race confident Tatsumaki would run a good race. We have been saying he is a nice horse but he is going the right way. He has got a great mind but we didn't think he would do it that easily as in a big field you don't know what is going to happen. Neil [Callan, jockey] said to me he would keep it simple. He has been saying for a long time that this is a Group horse. He has had so much confidence in the horse and he has always liked him.' The way he pulled clear in the closing stages suggested he'll be just as effective back at 7f and there's enough in his pedigree (his dam was a Listed winner over 1m) to suggest that he'll be well worth a try over the Guineas trip. Even if he doesn't stay 1m, he'd be a likely type for something like the Jersey Stakes at Royal Ascot and connections would also have the option of a return to sprint distances. Whatever the case, he's a strong, good-bodied sort – just the type to train on – and he's one to look forward to in 2022. MARCO BOTTI

TENEBRISM (USA)

3 bb f Caravaggio - Immortal Verse (Pivotal)

One of the most impressive performances of 2022 was spring maiden winner Tenebrism negotiating both a lengthy absence and the huge step up in grade when beating several more experienced fillies in the Group 1 Cheveley Park in October on only her second start. Admittedly market leader Sacred Bridge was disappointing and Tenebrism had the stands' rail to help in the last quarter-mile but that shouldn't detract in any way from the performance of the Aidan O'Brien filly, who showed a tremendous turn of foot to beat a progressive type in Flotus, who had got first run and momentarily looked like the winner when quickening a few lengths clear going into the dip. However, Tenebrism showed a fine turn of foot herself and she sustained it to such an effect that Ryan Moore, her rider, was able to win a shade snugly in the end. Following the race O'Brien stated, 'I didn't think it was possible to do it, not because of ability but because of the lay-off she had. Tenebrism had a setback after the last day and was off for a long time. She was just literally ready to come racing and I had a knot in my stomach whether it was fair to be running her or not, but there is only one Cheveley Park and you don't get horses with speed and the turn of foot she has very often and that is why she is here really. I had her in a 7f race at the weekend and usually if they get seven they will get a mile. You have to treat her as a Guineas filly but she could come back any time. She went to the line very strong and she is an exciting filly.' On this evidence she will almost certainly stay 7f and there's every chance she'll stay 1m (dam won in Group 2 and twice in Group 1 company over 1m). Her trainer has had a stranglehold on the English 1,000 Guineas, winning five of the last six runnings, and victory for this filly will take her trainer's winning record in the race to eight – just one off the overall record set by Robert Robson early in the 19th century. AIDAN O'BRIEN

THUNDER MAX
3 ch c Night Of Thunder - Tuolumne Meadows (High Chaparral)

It's reasonable to assume that Thunder Max didn't handle soft ground at Pontefract when he was upped in grade to Listed company on his second and final start of 2021, which came in mid-October. He had looked one to keep on the right side when scoring on good to firm on his debut five weeks earlier at the St Leger meeting at Doncaster. Over that 7f trip at Town Moor, he showed his inexperience throughout the contest but he made up plenty of ground in the last quarter-mile to hit the front in the closing stages and to win going away. That looked a useful effort and the race has had a few boosts from the subsequent wins of several that finished down the field. That debut performance prompted Richard Hannon, his trainer, to say, 'Thunder Max has always been a lovely colt. He was coming here for a run, he's not shown loads at home but quite often the good horses do that. He'll improve massively.' And, while he didn't do that at Pontefract, the ground was a huge mitigating factor (though it's worth noting his sire Night Of Thunder gets plenty of soft-ground winners) and he'll be well worth another chance as a 3-y-o. There is stamina on the dam's side so he should prove effective over middle distances and there's enough about him physically to suggest he'll train on and make up into a smart sort.
RICHARD HANNON

TUESDAY (IRE)
3 b f Galileo - Lillie Langtry (Danehill Dancer)

A full sister to the 2016 Epsom Oaks winner Minding as well as last season's Irish 1,000 Guineas heroine Empress Josephine, Tuesday was just seen once last season but she gave notice that she could be up to emulating those illustrious siblings as she resumes her career at three. She finished second of 14 to Discoveries in a 7f maiden at the Curragh in June, beaten a short head, with the Raceform race-reader saying afterwards that she 'would have to be fancied to turn tables on the winner should they meet again. She came off the bridle 2f out, was green and it took

some time for the penny to drop, but she kept on to good effect. She will come into her own over 1m+ in due course.' The filly who beat her had the benefit of previous experience and she would go on to win the Group 1 Moyglare Stud Stakes over the same C&D in September, while the third home that day, Mise Le Meas, beaten around 3l, would also boost the form by winning her maiden next time. Minding was well beaten in her maiden in 2015 and she went on to win five Group 1s, so there is plenty to be optimistic about, despite her defeat. Tuesday wasn't seen again but she's already been nibbled at for the Oaks, although there is still 25-1 available at the time of writing, which looks tempting.
AIDAN O'BRIEN

UNCLE BRYN

4 b g Sea The Stars - Wall Of Sound (Singspiel)

There could still be Pattern races to be won in 2022 with this gelded son of Sea The Stars, who has shown plenty of ability in just six career starts spread over two seasons. He won both his outings on the AW in late 2020 and then ran a fair race on his 2021 return when finishing third behind Wirko in the Blue Riband Trail at Epsom in April, with John Gosden saying afterwards, 'Uncle Bryn was coltish in proceedings and looking at everything. He will come on a lot mentally for the run.' However, his next start in May was a bit of a disaster as he finished last of nine in the Dante Stakes at York, where he was slowly away, took a firm grip and then faded tamely after losing his action. He was gelded after that run and returned 113 days later at Ascot, where he dictated a Class 2 handicap to win a shade cosily off an official mark of 99. He was next seen in the Cambridgeshire at Newmarket under a penalty and he was far from disgraced in that as he finished sixth of the 26 runners, having led until over a furlong out. Those two runs in September give cause for optimism and there's every chance that he can win a handicap off his current rating of 102, especially if he is allowed to dictate matters. After that, he could easily still develop into a Pattern-level performer.
JOHN & THADY GOSDEN

ZELLIE (FR)

3 b f Wootton Bassett - Sarai (Nathaniel)

Four wins, including a Group 1 at the end of the season, plus two second places from six outings is a fantastic return for this daughter of leading sire Wootton Bassett out of a half-sister to 1,000 Guineas winner Speciosa in her juvenile season and she could be an interesting outsider for the 1,000 Guineas should it come up soft or heavy at Newmarket in May. She was a convincing winner of the Prix Marcel Boussac over 1m at Longchamp (heavy) and her trainer Andre Fabre said afterwards, 'I'm delighted and I never thought Zellie would only be a two-year-old. She has the scope and ability to be nice next year. We're impatient to see her in the Guineas or the Poule d'Essai. I think she'll be limited to a mile, maybe the mile and a quarter of the Prix de Diane. There'll be no marathons for her.' Speciosa won the 1,000 Guineas on soft ground in 2006 and Zellie's sire Wootton Bassett also acted on ground with cut (he won the Prix Jean-Luc Lagardere on heavy ground in 2010) so it would appear that soft ground will be a minimum requirement for Zellie. Given her trainer's comments, she'd make no appeal for the Oaks, for which she is a 25-1 shot in the ante-post lists but she would make plenty of each-way appeal for either the English or French Guineas if conditions were suitable. ANDRE FABRE

INDEX

NOTES

NOTES

NOTES

100 WINNERS
JUMPERS TO FOLLOW
2022-23

Companion volume to *100 Winners: Horses to Follow - Flat*, this book discusses the past performances and future prospects of 100 horses, selected by Raceform's expert race-readers, that are likely to perform well in the 2022-23 jumps season. To order post the coupon to the address below or order online from **www.racingpost.com/shop**

Tel 01933 304858

ORDER FORM

Please send me a copy of **100 WINNERS: JUMPERS TO FOLLOW 2022-23** as soon as it is published. I enclose a cheque made payable to Pitch Publishing Ltd for **£6.99** (inc p&p)

Name (block capitals) ....

Address ....

....

Postcode ....

SEND TO: PITCH PUBLISHING,

SANDERS ROAD, WELLINGBOROUGH, NORTHANTS NN8 4BX